Baskets
and Basketry

Baskets and Basketry

by Dorothy Wright
Instructor in Crafts to the London County Council

Drawings by David Button

DAVID & CHARLES : NEWTON ABBOT

ISBN 0 7153 5472 8

First published in 1959 by B.T. Batsford Ltd
This edition published in 1972 by
David & Charles (Publishers) Limited
South Devon House Newton Abbot Devon

Reprinted 1974

© Dorothy Wright 1959, 1972
All rights reserved. No part of this
publication may be reproduced, stored
in a retrieval system, or transmitted
in any form or by any means, electronic,
mechanical, photocopying, recording or
otherwise, without the prior permission
of David & Charles (Publishers) Limited

Printed in Great Britain by
Redwood Burn Limited
Trowbridge & Esher

CONTENTS

	page
LIST OF PLATES	7
ACKNOWLEDGEMENT	9

1 INTRODUCTION 10
The Scope of the Book—The Industry—The Amateur—The Future

2 TECHNIQUE 22
Willow or Osier—Cane—Tools for Cane Basketry—Tools for Willow Basketry—Weaves—Decorative Weaves—Bases—Borders—Handles—Lids and Ledges—Notches—Ties and Trimmings—Construction of a Round Frame Basket

3 DESIGN 79
General—The Design of an Actual Basket

4 RECIPES 99
Wastepaper Basket—Simple Round Work-basket—Round Work-basket—Tall Oval Shopping Basket—Large Shopping Basket—All-purpose Plate—Swedish Plate—Lidded Picnic Basket—Wine Cradle—Round Linen Basket—Handbag with Leather Handles—Miniature Cradle—Miniature Round Shopping Basket—Carpet Beater—Bread or Fruit Bowl—Cane Rattle—Ball—Interlaced Dish—Interlaced Mat—Light Frame Shopping Basket—Oval Frame-type Dish

5 NOTES ON THE PHOTOGRAPHS 129
Fishing Baskets—Agricultural Baskets—Trade and Domestic—Toys—Design

6 BASKETMAKER'S VOCABULARY 135

7 BOOKS 137

APPENDIX A 139
Dyeing for Basket Makers

INDEX 142

LIST OF PLATES

facing page

The Silchester Basket	11
The Airborne Pannier	11
Professional Basketmaker working a Border	12
Quarter-Cran Herring Basket	15
Traditional Fish Creel and Baskets from Arbroath	16
Scottish Sculls	19
Coarse Fishing Basket	19
Fish Caizie from Orkney	19
Fly-Fishing Creel	20
Yarmouth Herring Swills	23
Eel Traps	23
Potato Basket, Monmouth	24
Garden Basket, Wales	67
Malt Skip	67
Huck-Muck	67
Fruit Picker	67
Oval Shopper	68
Egg Basket	73
Cat Basket	73
Bottle Basket	73
Log Basket	74
Skye Hen or Ose Basket	77
Work Basket	77
Shoe Basket, Hebrides	78
Tray	81
Tea Basket	82
Creelagh, Highlands and Islands of Scotland	82
Birdcage	83
Cradle	84
Willow Rattle	87
Doll's Chair and Sofa	87
Doll's Cradle	87
Plant Pot Holders	88
The Gainsborough	88
Heavy and Bulky Shopper in Cane, Plastic and Raffia	88
Wastepaper Basket	95
Simple Round Workbasket	96
Round Workbasket in Cane and Buff Willow	97
Tall Oval Shopping Basket	98
Large Shopping Basket	105
All-purpose Plate	106
Swedish Plate in Cane and Buff Willow	106
Lidded Picnic Basket	107
Wine Cradle	108

Round Linen Basket 109
Strong Shopping Basket 109
Miniatures: Cradle, Shopping Basket and Carpet Beater 110
Bread or Fruit Bowl and Cane Rattle 110
Ball, Interlaced Dish and Mat 111
Light Frame Shopping Basket and Frame Dish 112

ACKNOWLEDGEMENT

When this book was first published in 1959 I acknowledged a debt to W. G. Trust of the Rural Industries Bureau, without whose help with both text and photographs it could not have come into being. Since that time the Rural Industries Bureau has changed its name to the Council of Small Industries in Rural Areas—CoSIRA for short—and widened its scope. Mr Trust is still with the Council, ally and friend of all basketmakers and willow growers.

David Button, the brilliant student whose drawings do so much to teach hand and eye the techniques of the craft, is now an architect and lecturer. My debt to him remains endless.

Other good friends and helpers have passed on in the ensuing years, in particular Dr Evelyn Baxter, the Scottish ornithologist and author, whose unique collection of baskets of the Highlands and Islands of Scotland is now in safe keeping at the Shandwick Place gallery of the National Museum of Antiquities of Scotland in Edinburgh. Some professional basketmakers themselves have also left us, notably William Shelley of Salisbury. Others have retired. Leslie Maltby now lives and works near Canterbury. Primavera is no longer in London but sells baskets with other craftwork in King's Parade, Cambridge.

Many of the baskets illustrated here may now be seen at the Museum of English Rural Life at Reading University where a unique reference collection illustrating the basketmaker's craft has been created.

February 1972   DOROTHY WRIGHT

1. INTRODUCTION

IN THE FIRST place this book is intended for the amateurs of basketmaking, for those who love good baskets and for those who cultivate basketmaking as a recreation and a pleasure. Many of us need to use our hands in a creative way and without this we feel incomplete and deprived of a part of our humanity. In a world increasingly given over in its leisure time to looking on at others playing games, pursuing the arts or just endeavouring to entertain the rest of us, the crafts hold a satisfaction as old as man himself, the satisfaction of moulding a natural material with one's hands. So many factors come into this: the development of the five senses, an exploration of a special facet of one's own personality, the finding of a peculiar calm and contentment in a noisy world.

In all the crafts to some extent the sense is tactile, in basketmaking particularly so—a reason why it can be followed by the blind whose sense of touch must be developed above all the others. But to the rest of us the training of the eye is just as important (here the blind must use special rulers and aids), and hand and eye work in unison to create a shape, to think and form it far more slowly than a potter shapes a pot. The damp clay can quickly be squeezed back into a lump to be re-formed on the wheel, but for the basketmaker to undo laborious hours of weaving because the whole does not please the dream of symmetry in his inner eye is a stronger test of character! The reworked job well done completes the satisfaction there is in being able to say "I made that" and without apology.

Basketmaking is still a profession in many countries. A century ago thousands made it their living, now the numbers have shrunk to hundreds. Because the best baskets are made by these professionals, this book contains many pictures of traditional working baskets. Many are, of course, outside the scope of the amateur as they stand, because he is seldom able to obtain or to work with basket willows. But their shape can be followed and copied in cane and so it is hoped that, by looking and borrowing, the amateur may be led to create new baskets for new needs as has always been the case. Sections 2 and 3 on TECHNIQUE and DESIGN set out the ways in which such baskets can be made and though these sections are mainly intended for the amateur it is hoped that the information in them will prove useful to professional workers too, particularly to the younger ones whose training is not as detailed as it used to be.

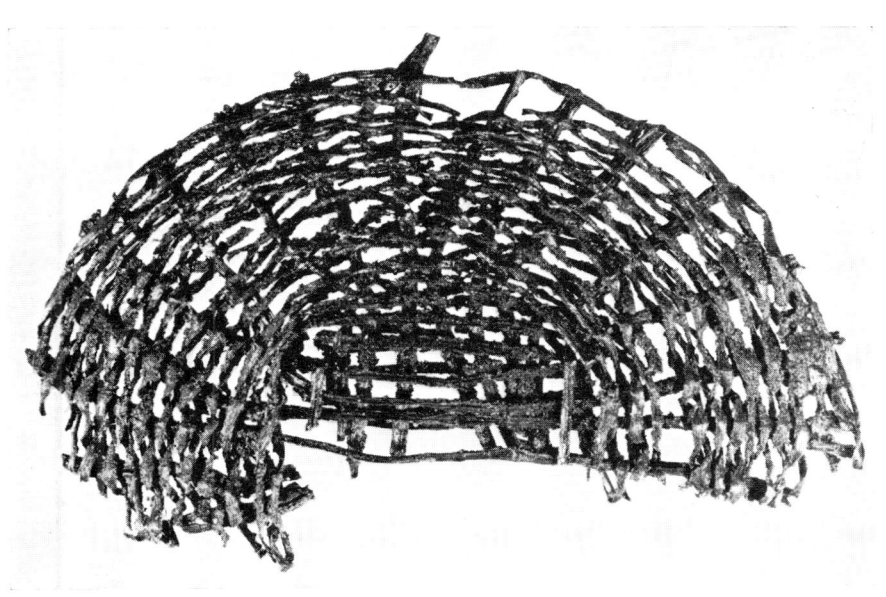

1   The Silchester Basket (*see page 129*)

2   The Airborne Pannier (*see page 129*)

3 Professional Basketmaker working a Border (*see page 129*)

INTRODUCTION

It is not extravagant to claim basketry as the earliest artifact. The first human being who wove branches together to make a shelter began it. Basketry has been called the mother of pottery, since baskets were used as molds for cooking pots by the Indians of the south western United States, particularly in Arizona and New Mexico, dating from 5,000 to 1,000 B.C. Their graves have yielded great quantities of baskets which, though made in the first instance for domestic use, provide an example of one of the wonders and mysteries of the human race—the creation of a pure art form by primitive people, in this case always women. This art was identified with religion, and sacred symbols were woven into baskets used in ceremonies of birth, death and marriage and the baskets themselves became sacred. Baskets were in fact used in sacred ceremonies all over the ancient world as well as for domestic use: and by traders and travellers. This last is one reason why patterns and weaves became so universal. Willow baskets from Italy or Scandinavia show the same weaves and techniques as cane ones from China, and it is hard to tell a sewn coil basket from Africa from one made in Malaya unless one is an expert.

Among more primitive peoples today great elaboration in plaiting and the use of dyes is still evident and miraculously fine woven mats and carrying baskets are still in daily use. These are sometimes exported and appear in craft shops and are worth study.

One may wonder why the craft industry of basketmaking is shrinking all over the world since the appreciation of the hand-made tends to grow. Baskets are first and foremost utilitarian things and because we live in an age of cardboard the wicker hamper once used in packing and transport has been largely superseded by the cardboard carton. The rapid advances made since the last war in the development of synthetic materials, light metal alloys, hardboards and plywood have changed the whole picture. In the great vegetable and flower markets of the western world today one does not see a single basket. Nevertheless there are still many in use in both country and town by builders, fishermen, agricultural workers, postmen, distributors of food and drink and in factories, potteries and on railways.

In medieval times every European village had its basketmaker who grew his materials, osiers or basket willows, on his own or a rented plot of land. The craft was very much a family affair, the women and children helping with the harvesting and processing of the willows and making baskets, mats and mattresses from rushes and reeds to supply the general need. They would take their wares to the weekly markets and build up stocks to sell at the great fairs when the stewards of the great houses, secular and religious, came to stock up for the whole year. Even now there are basketmaking families still at work, though the cultivation of willows tends to be a separate trade.

INTRODUCTION

Until 1925 the Shakers—a religious sect in the United States—were making exquisite baskets for sewing. In New England sturdy baskets of split ash are made to carry pies and cakes to church suppers. These resemble the veneer baskets of Scandinavia, having also a lid and tray.

There is still a considerable basketmaking industry in Western Germany centred round Lichtenfels and Michelau, possibly the biggest in Europe. The basketmakers work in their own homes and their produce is collected and marketed by merchants. There is a State School of Basketry here and a Basket Museum with a collection of over 500 baskets. Baskets are made in quantity in Poland and East Germany but here the workers have been gathered into factories run by the state. Basket willows are grown and exported from Poland, Jugoslavia and Bulgaria, all under the control of the state and the industry appears to be growing. Elsewhere in Europe it is in decline and though most basketmakers prefer their native materials they have to import osiers, some from far away. Britain gets many from Argentina and the Canary Islands as well as from Europe.

The Industrial Revolution changed the world of many basketmakers as it did the world of many craftsmen. 'Mills and factories brought a new demand for great hampers and crates to carry raw materials and components from one section to another, many being mounted on wheels. Fashion also has always played a part in the world of basketmaking and throughout the nineteenth century fine baskets became exceedingly popular and wicker furniture, always well made though somewhat florid in taste, was much used in Europe and the United States. Manufacturers' catalogues show a myriad chairs, sofas, tables, *jardinières* and the like with or without stuffed and buttoned cushions, and some still appear today as antiques.

By the end of the century the whole craft was prospering and some modest fortunes were made. Willow growers of course did well and cane began to be imported in quantity from South East Asia—the processing of the pith or centre cane we use today being developed about 1880.

Anyone who has tried to bend or work a thick willow rod or heavy cane will understand how very skilled professional basketmakers are (3). No one has ever invented a machine to make a basket and the maker's foremost tools are his hands. At a pinch he can make most baskets with nothing but a sharp knife. Such other tools as he uses are of the simplest. It is a pity that fewer young men are going into the industry; there is enough work to support many more and the pay is good. Piecework is the general rule and a skilled man can make a fair living. Training takes from three to five years and a good craftsman is invaluable to a master contractor and is spoken of with the highest appreciation and respect.

One of the chief dangers to the surviving basketmaker is an old one; the

4 Quarter-Cran Herring Basket (*see page 129*)

5 Traditional Fish Creel and Baskets from Arbroath (*see page 129*)

importation of cheap foreign basketware. It tends to come from places where the makers are paid little and can generally be recognised by those of us who make our own. The good strong simple willow basket has seldom come from overseas and surely it is worth paying a little more to get something that will not only wear longer but please the eye. We cannot ourselves, as amateurs, make log or dog baskets or rustic chairs and tables for the garden and these are things the professional basketmaker makes supremely well.

The last war brought an extraordinary demand for two million airborne panniers (2) to carry supplies to paratroops. Nearly every basketmaker in Britain was making these. The British army still uses a very fine willow pannier fitted with medical supplies. No substitute has been found for these baskets which wear longer, are repairable, and are better to use than fibre substitutes.

Basketmaking is an industry where the blind and the partially sighted can earn their own living. Since the 1914 war many blind have received a training in their association's workshops and become valuable members of the trade. Many have been able to set up independently. They do excellent cane chair seating. The blind workshops make hampers and baskets for fishing and agriculture.

The sedentary nature of the craft makes it suitable for some disabled people, but the variable demand may affect both blind and disabled who, because of their disabilities, cannot always turn to another type of basketware when the market changes. Naturally both these groups of workers have a slower rate of production than other professionals.

On the whole the industry seems to be going back to its roots, to the countryside where its materials grow and where conditions are kinder. But London is still the headquarters of The Worshipful Company of Basket-makers and in 1969 it celebrated the four hundredth anniversary of its foundation.

All baskets were not made by trained men in the past. By tradition the rougher sorts were made by the people who used them: farmers, farm workers, gipsies and fisherman (6, 8, 137). There are still small plantations of willows particularly near the south-western coasts of Britain which are cut for the making of lobster and crab pots and were used for farm baskets too. Most of these were probably of the frame type, a very ancient basket form.

Many baskets in Scotland have a very long ancestry. They are called creels and some are still carried on the back and on ponies in the remoter parts of the Isles, but to many a creel means a basket for fish. In the Isles only local material was used in the past: bents or oat straw and string for coiled baskets, and even heather and docken stalks for fish and peat baskets (8). The Aleutian Islanders weave their baskets with wild rye grass. Iceland has no forest trees

INTRODUCTION

at all yet so strong is the urge to make baskets that tiny things were made from the tough roots of birch and alpine willow. The Iroquois Indians of New York used plaited corn husks to make simple masks. Corn or maize leaves are also much used in the cornlands of Central Europe to make carrying baskets which are widely exported. In general the type of material available locally determines the type of basket technique in use and in part the sort of basket that is made. The countries of Eastern Asia: Indonesia, Malaysia, China and Japan, make their baskets mainly of cane and bamboo, both being split into every possible width and thickness. So versatile is the split and shaved bamboo that both hampers and flexible lace-like bags may be made. Needless to say these techniques are not explained in this book nor is the making of sewn coil baskets which may use any flexible material from straw, grass, raffia or cane.

THE AMATEUR

The making of baskets by women as a recreation was part of the Victorian passion for handwork. Rush and straw were plaited and woven and, in the latter half of the nineteenth century, cane stirred creative imaginations to new heights of invention because it provided a material that all women could use, our native willow being too hard for most female hands to cope with.

Old needlework encyclopaedias show a great variety of little baskets, some made at home but many imported from Germany, simply as vehicles or foundations for every sort of embroidery and trimming. They were smothered with beads, feathers, silk fringes and tassels, canvas or Berlin work, crochet and other incongruous delights. Much of the taste and fashion of that time seems strange to us now that every woman does her own cooking and housekeeping and has little time for elaborate needlework. We tend to make useful things for our homes, adding simple decoration for pleasure in the design and the learning of a new skill. The therapeutic value of basketwork has long been recognised in hospitals and rehabilitation centres and quite a few people go on making baskets as a recreation when they are well again. Much good light basketware is made in women's and evening classes all over the country. Nor have amateurs only worked for pleasure: in the 1914 war, village classes helped the war effort by making shell cases and in the last war the British Women's Institutes made 5,200 potato baskets.

THE FUTURE

On the professional side there is no sign of a falling-off in the need or the public demand for basketware. The cry in all busy workshops is for younger men to go into the industry. While the main output will always be commer-

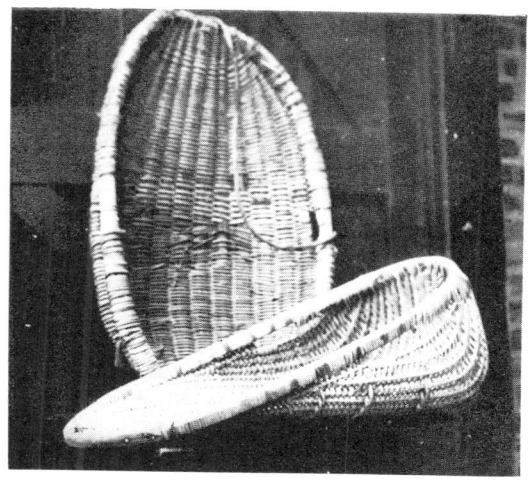

6 Scottish Sculls
(*see page 130*)

7 Coarse Fishing Basket
(*see page 130*)

8 Fish Caizie from Orkney
(*see page 130*)

9 Fly-Fishing Creel *(see page 130)*

cial there is no doubt that there is money to be made by producing the more interesting traditional baskets for use in new domestic ways. Perhaps it is surprising that such practical objects as baskets are subject to the whims of women's fashions, but there is no doubt that short skirts do not agree with shopping baskets and wicker furniture because of the danger to nylon. When skirts come down again, wicker will come back into fashion.

A major problem is the conviction in the public mind that baskets ought to be cheap. The purchaser neither knows nor cares that the cultivation and harvesting of osiers or basket willows anywhere in the world is specialised and skilled agricultural work to be paid for by a fair wage and return, nor that cane cutters in south-east Asia are beginning to demand a higher standard of living. Freight charges (cane comes halfway round the world) and other overheads have forced up the price of this material. The amateur knows this too. On the whole, we are becoming educated to the idea that time is valuable and it is fair to pay more for handmade things. We do not argue about paying a little more for a hand woven scarf or a hand-blocked print or a hand-thrown pot, so why not for a basket?

2. TECHNIQUE

Materials for Basketmaking

WILLOW or OSIER

THERE are many varieties of willows (*Salix*) growing all over the world; the most important species used in basketry are:

(a) *Salix triandra*, which produces high quality rods an average of 7 ft. long. The most important variety of this willow is Black Maul.
(b) *Salix viminalis* gives a stouter type of rod, up to 12 ft. long, which is used in coarser basketry such as hurdles and agricultural baskets.
(c) *Salix purpurea*, which is not much grown now. It gives a small, slender, very tough rod up to 4 ft. long, which buffs well and was used for small high-class basketware such as luncheon baskets.

LOCALITY AND CONDITIONS

There is an old saying that "land that will bear fat beasts will bear good willows". The main willow-growing area in England is now in Somerset, in the rich alluvial "moors" drained by the rivers Parrett, Yeo and Tone. The main centre is Langport and the Paddington–Penzance railway line runs through the willow beds, so that any interested traveller can see the industry being carried on.

The moors are flat and have to be well drained by a maze of ditches, because of seasonal flooding. Modern pumping stations have greatly improved the drainage.

Willows need rich, deep and well-drained soil, especially clay and silt mixtures. There must be abundant water and good drainage, though *Salix viminalis* will grow in poor soil and *Salix purpurea* in a sandy soil.

In the past, willows were also grown in large numbers in Lancashire, the Trent Valley, in Nottingham and East Anglia, but since 1925 the areas of land under willow-cultivation has decreased everywhere except in Somerset. Wild willows are said to have no "nature", or if they have, it is not "kind".

10　Yarmouth Herring Swills (*see page 130*)

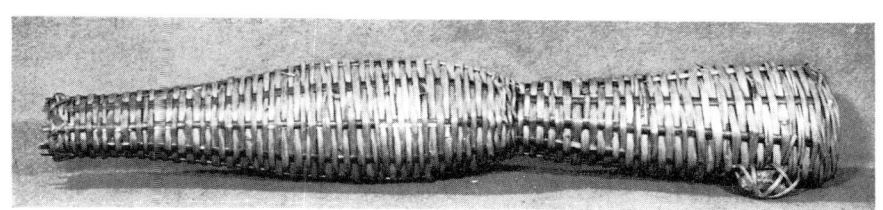

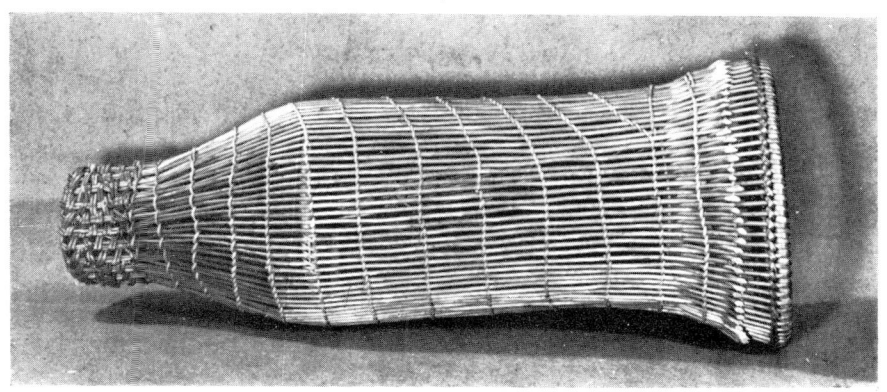

11, 12　Eel Traps (*see page 130*)

13 Potato Basket, Monmouth (*see page 130*)

TECHNIQUE

"Nature" may be defined as strength and elasticity—a good skein has such a nature that you could lace your boots with it. "Kindness" is harder to define, but any worker with willow or cane knows what it means. One might call it co-operation.

CULTIVATION

The life of a willow bed varies from twenty to fifty years, and the first saleable crop is obtained in the third season after planting.

Planting is usually done in March or April, in clean land. Cuttings or sets 9–15 ins. in length are made from one-year-old rods, and pushed into the ground until approximately one-third of their length is showing, buds upward. Rows are carefully measured, and a space of 27 ins. between each row and 14 ins. between cuttings allows room for power-driven cultivators. One acre so spaced requires about 16,500 cuttings.

During the first two seasons after planting the new bed must be carefully and frequently weeded. The shoots are cut annually in winter and early spring to encourage new growth.

A mature bed also requires weeding but no fertiliser, because of the heavy leaf-fall.

Harvesting is done annually, any time during the winter or spring before the sap rises. Cutting is a highly skilled job done with a heavy sickle. Rods are tied into bundles, and an acre yields an average of 200 bundles.

PROCESSING AND MARKETING

In the autumn willow auctions are held. Some growers sell their uncut standing crop, others sell it harvested and processed. The buyer of an uncut crop undertakes to cut it by the following spring. No exact figures can be given, but 54 acres of willows were auctioned for £90 an acre in 1953.

After cutting, the bundles of willows are graded by standing them in a tub and selecting them against a measuring stick. The rods are graded in foot-lengths from 3 ft. upwards.

Brown Willows are rods dried and used with the bark on.

White Willows are rods peeled without boiling just before they break into leaf. In most cases bundles for "peeling for white" are "pitted", that is: stood in 6 ins. of water, either in ditches or concrete pits. In spring they begin to break into leaf and can be peeled.

Buff Willows are brown rods that have been boiled in tanks for several hours and then peeled, giving a red-brown colour.

Peeling used to be done by hand, but the bulk of the crop is now machine-peeled, only a few whites being done by hand. In both cases a device called

TECHNIQUE

a willow-brake is used. Two smooth metal rods are sprung together and the willow rod is drawn between them, stripping off the bark. After peeling, the rods are dried in the open air spread out along hedges, fences and walls, a characteristic sight throughout the willow country.*

IMPORTED WILLOWS

Insufficient willows are grown in England today to supply basketmakers. West Country baskets are mostly made of Somerset willows, but basketmakers in the cities in Scotland, the Midlands and East Anglia, if they are unable to get local willows, are compelled to use imported ones.

Excellent white or buff willows are coming in from Spain, the Netherlands, the Argentine, Belgium, Poland, Portugal, Madeira, Austria, Hungary, Germany and the Irish Republic.

These willows are often better graded and cheaper than Somerset willows, but there is no doubt that English basketmakers prefer native material when they can get it. They are, however, independent and tough, and as one East Anglian man said, "I will buy good stuff from anywhere." The Rural Industries Bureau is doing much to encourage the recultivation of old willow beds, but bad summers and the recent East Coast floods, together with the high cost of labour, do not make things easier.

PREPARATION FOR WORKING WITH WILLOWS

Materials should be sorted and prepared beforehand. Bottom sticks should be thicker than stakes; wale rods a little thinner than stakes; siding material half the thickness of the stakes. In fine work 18-in. to 2-ft. rods will be used for weaving, and 3-ft., 4-ft. and 5-ft. rods for stakes and sticks.

Willows are worked in a damp or mellow condition, which means that they must be soaked in cold or warm water (never hot) and then allowed to lie in a cool place.

The times for soaking vary according to the thickness and type of willow and are largely gauged by experience. A rough table is:

Brown Rods
Luke (from 3 ft.–4 ft. 6 ins.)	2–3 days
Long Small (from 4 ft. 6 ins.–5 ft. 6 ins.)	3–4 days
Threepenny and Middleboro' (from 5 ft. 6 ins.–8 ft.)	4–5 days
Great (from 8 ft.–9 ft.)	1 week

* See *Cultivation and Uses of Basket Willows*, by K. G. Stott, B.Sc., Willow Officer, Unit of Bristol Research Station, Long Ashton, Bristol.

TECHNIQUE

White and Buff

Tacks (2 ft. 6 ins.–3 ft. 6 ins.)	$\frac{1}{4}$–$\frac{1}{2}$ hour
Small and Long Small (3 ft. 6 ins.–6 ft.)	$\frac{1}{2}$–1 hour
Threepenny and Middleboro'	2–3 hours
Great	3–4 hours
Skeins	merely dipped

In all cases, the stuff, after being taken from the water, should be laid down in a sheltered place for a night or some hours to mellow, care being taken not to prepare more white or buff than is needed for one or two days' work.*

Skeining is the use of thin strips of the inner skin of willows. (See WILLOW TOOLS, page 33.)

CANE

Calamus. Cane or rattan is the generic name for the many varieties of cane palm, growing in the jungle and virgin forest of tropical countries. No cane grows in the British Isles, exept at Kew. The trade names of the best known varieties used in industry are:

FIG. 14

Tohiti. A thick cane 12 mm. to 30 mm. in diameter, used for furniture.

Malacca. The cane associated with walking sticks and umbrella handles. Also used for furniture frames.

Kubu. A yellow soft-natured variety, used for heavy industrial baskets, from 5 mm. to 12 mm. in diameter.

Palembang. A small smooth reddish cane 3 mm. to 8 mm. in diameter, tougher than processed cane and useful for smaller hampers and industrial baskets. It splits well and can be used by the amateur in this state.

Sarawak and *Segah.* The varieties from which chair seating and centre canes are manufactured.

Whangee. The nobbed yellow cane popular for umbrella and bag handles.

CULTIVATION

The best cane grows in Malaya, Borneo, Sarawak, Java and Celebes. It is also found in Burma, Indo-China, Australia, Africa and China. The plant cannot be said to be cultivated as it grows wild and needs no attention. Single canes grow to enormous lengths, up to 600 ft., but the average diameter is about 1 in. It is difficult to harvest because the outer skin is covered with hooked thorns. Natives work in heavy gloves with axes. After

* From *The Art of Basketmaking*, Thomas Okey.

TECHNIQUE

cutting, the canes are left to dry where they grew and the spiny covering can then be stripped off. The inner bark, shiny and hard, is the surface we know in glossy lapping, and chair cane.

After the outer bark is removed the canes are cut into 12–30-ft. lengths, tied in bundles, and sent by water to Singapore, which is the world centre for cane production and marketing.

MARKETING

From Singapore cane is shipped all over the world, through intermediaries in London and Singapore.

PROCESSING

The preparation of centre cane, lapping and chair seating canes is rarely carried out in this country. Holland, Germany and America have become the main centres of the industry. After washing, the outer surface is split off by machine and this is made into various thicknesses and grades of lapping and chair-seating cane. The tough cream fibrous core is known in this country as "pulp" or "centre" cane, in Australia as pith or rattan-core, and in the United States as reed. It is cut with circular knives into various diameters sold in this country by numbers ranging from 000 to 15. The measures are in millimetres, and the following table may be useful in copying foreign pattern books.

Centre Cane No.	Mm. Size
1	$1\frac{3}{4}$
2	$1\frac{7}{8}$
3	2
4	$2\frac{1}{4}$
5	$2\frac{1}{2}$
6	$2\frac{5}{8}$
7	$2\frac{3}{4}$
8	3
9	$3\frac{1}{4}$
10	$3\frac{3}{8}$
11	$3\frac{1}{2}$
12	$3\frac{3}{4}$
14	$4\frac{1}{4}$
16	5

Handle cane for basketry does not have a number and may be bought from 4 mm. to 8 mm. in centre cane, and from 6 mm. to 10 mm. in glossy.

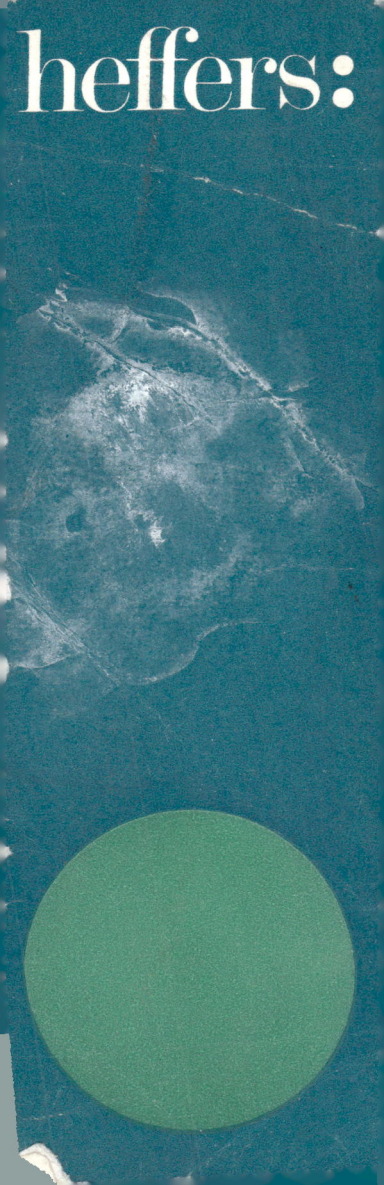

heffers:
Booksellers & Publishers
20 Trinity Street Cambridge
Telephone (0223) 58351

TECHNIQUE

Chair-seating canes run from No. 1 (very fine) to No. 6, and are usually sold in two grades: Red and White Tie, both Continental.

(1 metre = 39·37 ins.)
(1 millimetre = 0·039 in.)

GRADING AND QUALITY

The main divisions of quality of centre canes are "Continental" and "Far East" or "Hong Kong". The buyer knows the grade by the colour of the string with which each pound bundle is tied. Continental is sold in Blue Tie and Red Tie, the latter being satisfactory for all but exhibition work. Far East is sold in Red Tie and White Tie, and occasionally Yellow and Black Tie. The quality is inferior to Continental cane, though a Far Eastern Red Tie can be used for class work and all grades are used commercially.

Since the war, West German processing firms have invented a method of bleaching the dark portions of the cane core which previously were unusable for basketry. This renders the cane very soft, more like macaroni when damp. This may be an advantage in therapy, but the resulting work is neither strong nor lively to look at and has a dead antiseptic air. It colours with age just as cream cane does, but it is cheaper.

PREPARATION

Long soaking of centre cane is to be deprecated. It spoils the quality and can even turn it black. Use damp weaving canes and if they dry, pass them through the water. Dry cane will not shape well.

Approximate Times in the Water

8-mm. and 5-mm. handle cane	20–30 minutes
Nos. 14–10	15 minutes
Nos. 9– 7	10 minutes
Nos. 6– 4	5 minutes
Nos. 3 and under	pass through water

N.B. Where it is possible to let the canes lie under a wet cloth or sack, soaking of the canes smaller than No. 9 will not be needed at all. They need simply to be dipped in water first.

It is a good rule not to wet stakes and liners after they have been upsett, unless a very marked curve is to be made, until the border is reached.

Palembang has a hard outer skin and requires several hours in the water, but when split the exposed core quickly absorbs water. Sizes 3–5 require 10–15 minutes. Lengths of palembang may be split by holding the cane

TECHNIQUE

under the left arm, making a split in the end with a knife and pulling the two pieces apart. When one splits thinner than the other, bend the thicker one away from it. This requires a little practice but is not difficult. Palembang makes a strong resilient basket. Split the cane when dry.

Shiny Handle Cane requires longer soaking than the matt sort.

Tools for Cane Basketry

The minimum essentials are marked *.

* 15. *Long Bodkin* for the insertion of handles.

16. *Medium Bodkin* for working borders, insertion of stakes, etc.

17. *Fine Bodkin* for fine work. The bodkin is in constant use and saves time and work.

* 18. *Round-nosed Pliers* for squeezing canes so that they may bend at an angle without cracking.

19. *Secateurs* for cutting handle and heavier cane.

* 20. *Knife* for slyping.

* 21. *Sidecutters* for all general cutting and picking.

22. *Rapping Iron* for tapping down weaving to keep it even.

* 23. *Ruler* for constant checking during work. A flexible steel rule is also useful.

24. *Hammer* for use in nailing handles, frames, etc.

25. *Cane Spirit Lamp* for singeing off the hairs on a cane basket after completion.

26. *Screw Block*, the foundation in making a rectangular base or lid. Shown in use in Fig. 58.

27. *Workboard*, the basket is pinned to it with 28, a *Bradawl*, and revolves in work. (See *Weights*, below.)

Extras:

Long-nosed Pliers will hold an end that fingers cannot reach, and are also useful in nailing.

Assorted Basketry Nails may be obtained in $\frac{1}{4}$-lb. packets of mixed sizes. Used in making frames and in nailing two or more handle bows together before lapping.

Weights. Where a workboard is unobtainable or unsuitable, a 1- or 2-lb. weight, an old hammer-head or even half a brick or a screw-top jar of water will steady a basket on the table.

TECHNIQUE

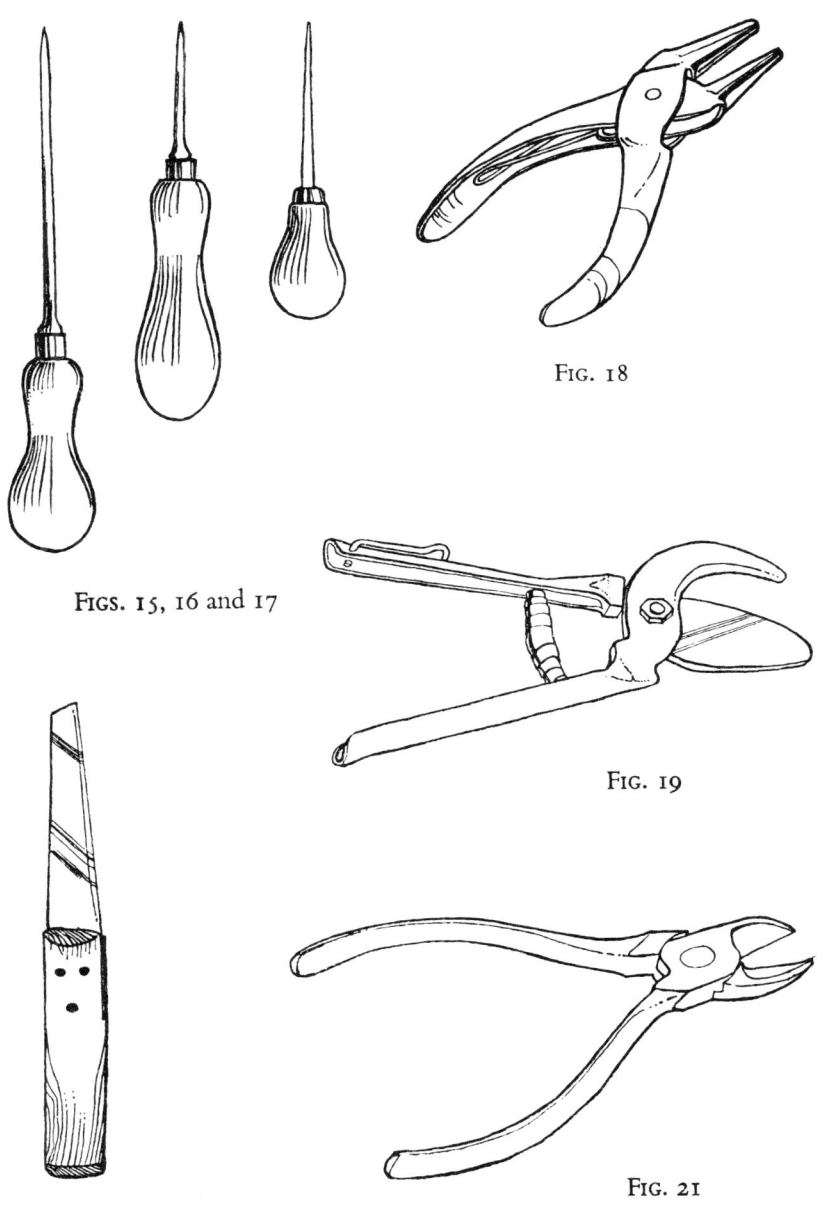

FIG. 18

FIGS. 15, 16 and 17

FIG. 19

FIG. 21

FIG. 20

TOOLS FOR CANE BASKETRY

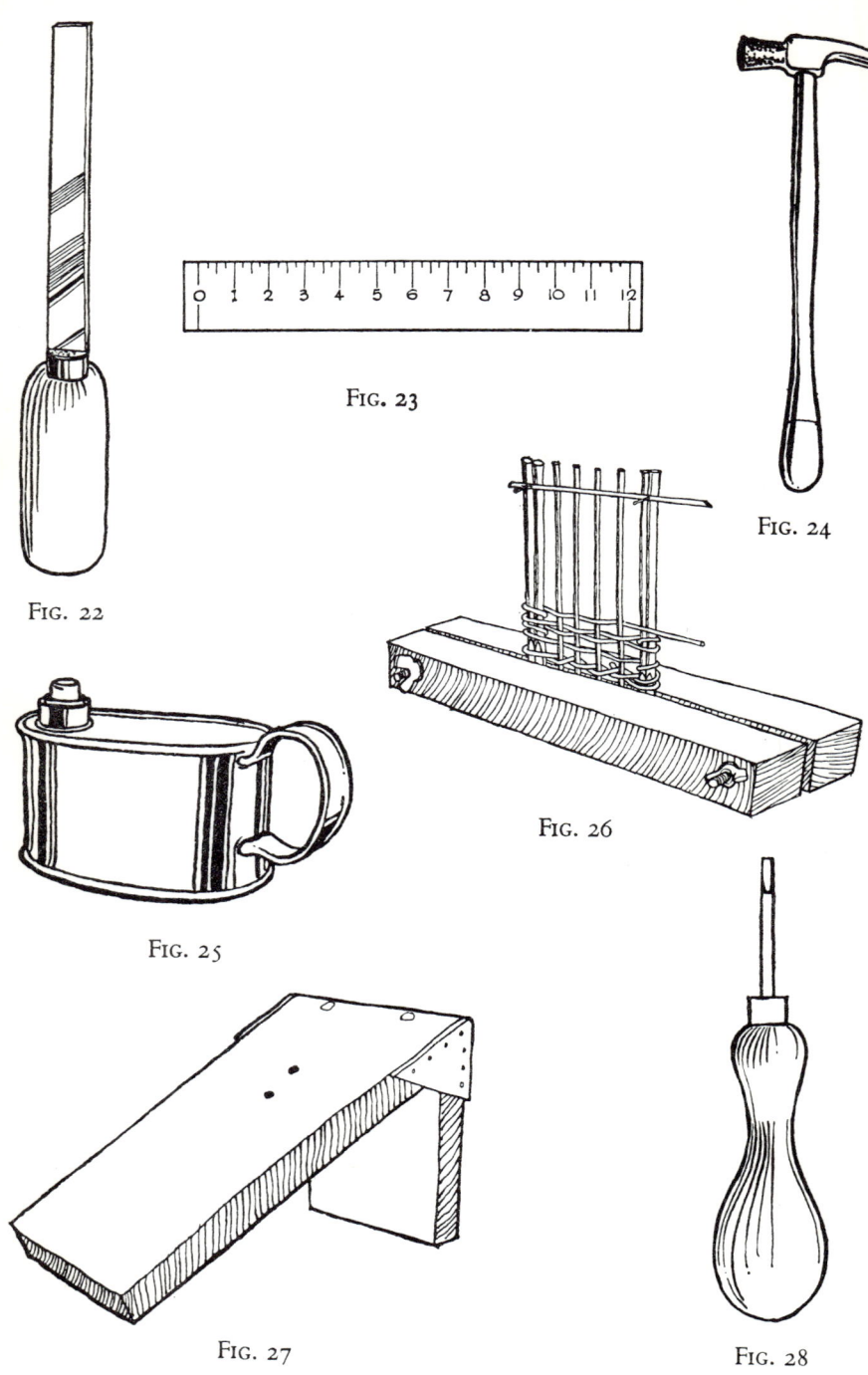

FIG. 22 FIG. 23 FIG. 24 FIG. 25 FIG. 26 FIG. 27 FIG. 28

TOOLS FOR CANE BASKETRY

TECHNIQUE

Clothes Pegs are a great help, particularly to the disabled, as a "third hand", when starting a large wale or as a guide to a starting place or one to be watched.

Jam Jar. It is helpful to rib-rand (37) a lid on the top of a jam jar. A good dome may be made and the lid swings round fast in weaving.

Selotape is a useful tie for fine work but will not hold on wet material.

Sharpening Stone for knives.

Soft Soap or Tallow. The bodkin is dipped in this before making a place for a handle or inserted into a rectangular base when staking-up.

String.

Tools for Willow Basketry

29. *Cleave* for splitting dry rods to make skeins. To make three clefts the cleave has three "fins". It is held in the right hand while the left hand guides the rod. The clefts run up through the fingers of the right hand.

30. *Shave.* The cleft is drawn through, pith side upwards, with the right hand, while the left hand holds it down on the far side of the blade. (A thumb guard should be worn.) First the butt end is shaved; then the cleft is turned and the rest shaved. The thickness of the skein is determined by the number of times it is taken through the shave and the adjustment of the blade by the screw.

31. *Upright.* When very fine and even skeins are wanted they are drawn

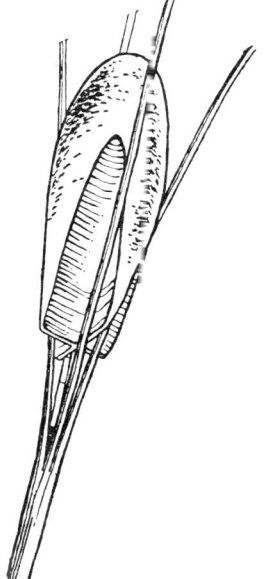

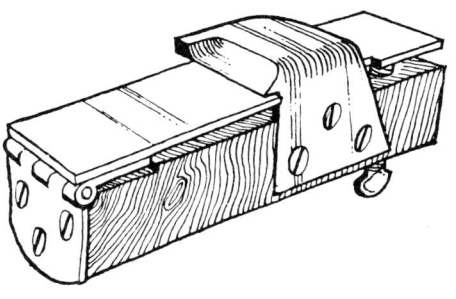

FIG. 29   FIG. 30

TECHNIQUE

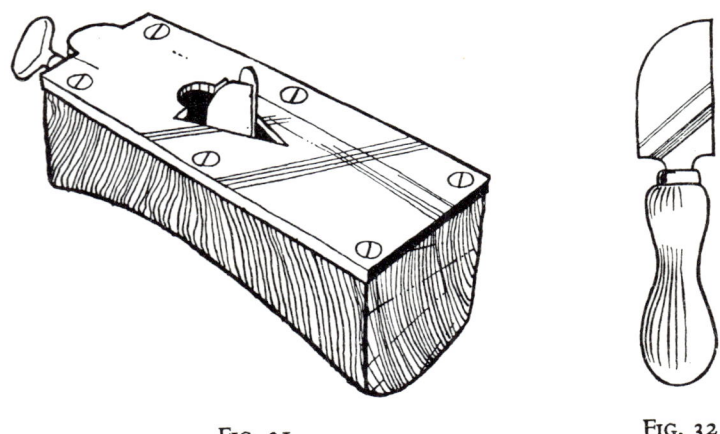

FIG. 31   FIG. 32

through the twin blades, which are adjusted by the screw. The skein is held in the same way as in the use of the shave. An uprighted skein has no butt or tip.

32. *Picking Knife.* The curved tip is used for picking.

The tools used in cane basketry and shown in Figs. 15–28 are used in willow work, with the exception of 17, 18, 21 and 25. Heavier shears than the pair shown at 19 are used, and a heavier iron than that at 22, but the illustrated tools will serve for fine willow work.

Weaves

Randing. (Cane) (33). To join, the old and new weavers lie behind the same stake. When randing with willow the butt of a rod is laid between

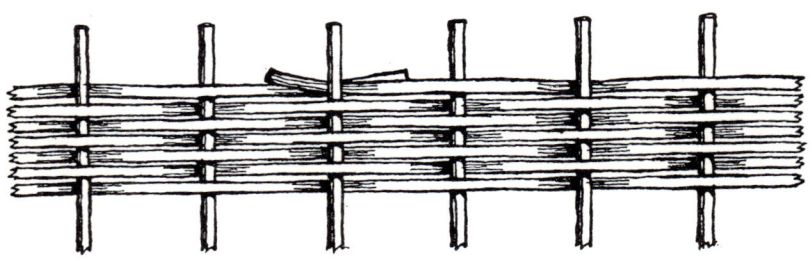

FIG. 33

TECHNIQUE

two stakes and worked over and under to its top. The next rod is laid in between the next stakes to the right and worked the same. This movement continues all the way up the side.

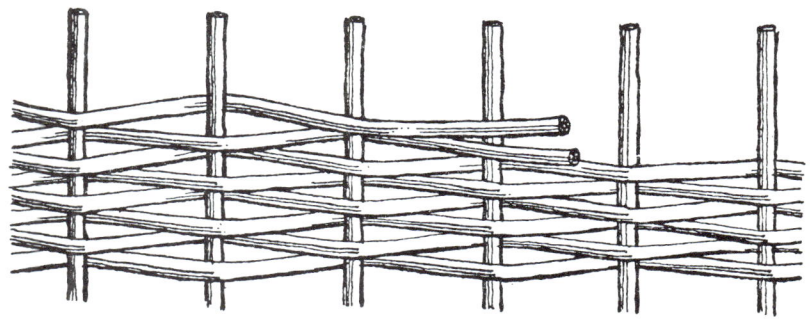

FIG. 34

In randing a square lid or bottom the rods are joined butt to tip, continuously.

Randing (34) with two weavers when there is an even number of stakes. Sometimes called "chasing".

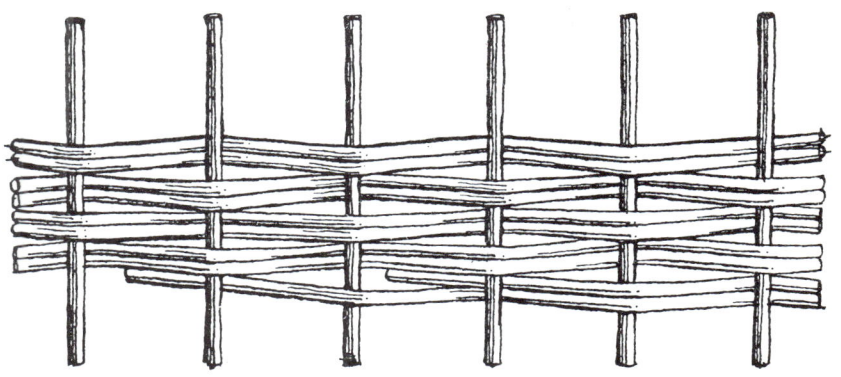

FIG. 35

Slewing (35). Randing with two or more weavers together. The start and the finish are graded so that there is no gap.

French Randing (36) is used in willow work. Each rod is laid in to the left

35

TECHNIQUE

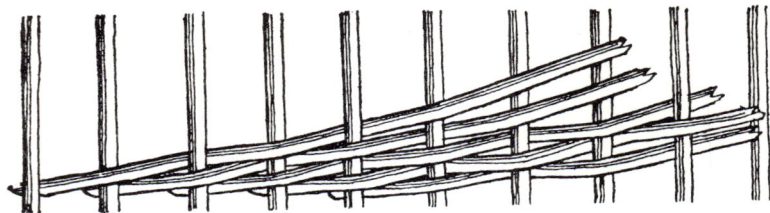

FIG. 36

of the previous one and one randing stroke worked. This is repeated over one stake and under the next with each weaver until they are worked out.

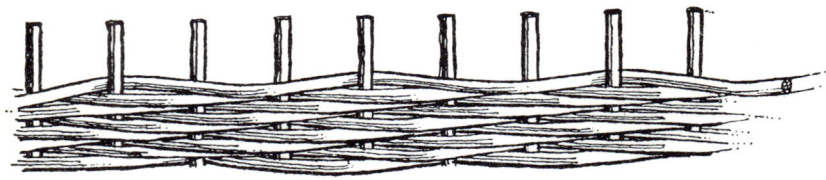

FIG. 37

Rib-randing (37) must be worked over a number of stakes not divisible by three. The close weave is useful on lids. Joining is the same as for simple randing.

FIG. 38

Three-rod Wale (38). Three weavers worked in sequence over any number of stakes. Joining-in new weavers or completing a band or single round of waling (39). In canework the canes are joined in singly as required.

FIG. 39

TECHNIQUE

Changing-the-stroke when working from one round of 3-rod wale to another, in canework. The movement is CBAA, as follows: when the leading cane C is lying behind stake No. 1 (40) it is worked in front of two

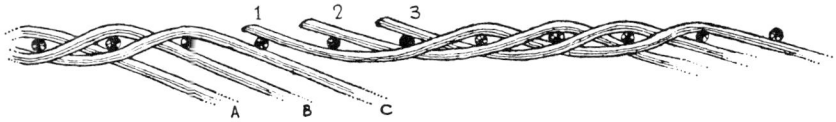

FIG. 40

stakes and behind one so that it is lying in front of stake No. 3. Then cane B is worked in front of two stakes and behind one, and then cane A the same. This completes the round. To bring A to the correct position for working the next round, it is worked again (41). The wale continues as before.

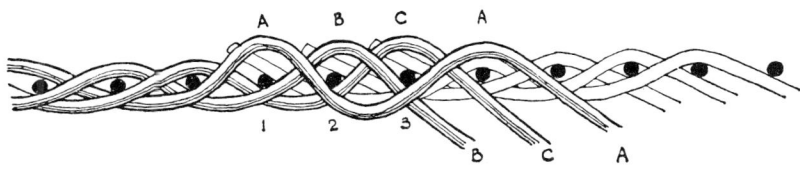

FIG. 41

The Change-of-stroke or change-over is worked every time a new round of waling is begun. Some workers mark stake No. 1 until they are able to recognise it.

FIG. 42

To complete the wale before going on to another weave, the change-over is *not* worked. A, B and C are worked in normal sequence when stake No. 1 is reached and are either left at the back of the work or brought through to the front so that the movement is uninterrupted (42).

37

TECHNIQUE

To *change-over* from a 4-*rod* to a 3-*rod* wale, work the back weaver A in front of three and behind one when the start is reached; it will then lie on top of weaver 1. Cut off. With the remaining three weavers work D, C, B in front of three and behind one and they will be in position to work a 3-rod wale and can be called A, B and C.

FIG. 43

4-*rod* *Wale* (43). If four weavers are worked in front of two and behind two the weave looks like a 3-rod wale on both sides. This is useful in working strong bands of colour or on a bowl-shape where both sides are clearly visible, and is also a good weave for a base.

4-, 5- *and* 6-*rod* *Wales* are usually worked with four, five and six weavers, going in front of three, four and five and behind one, respectively, though it is possible to vary the stroke to serve a particular purpose.

A change-of-stroke may be used with any number of waling canes remembering that it will always begin with the leading weaver and at the first stake. The formula for a 5-rod change-over would be EDCBAA.

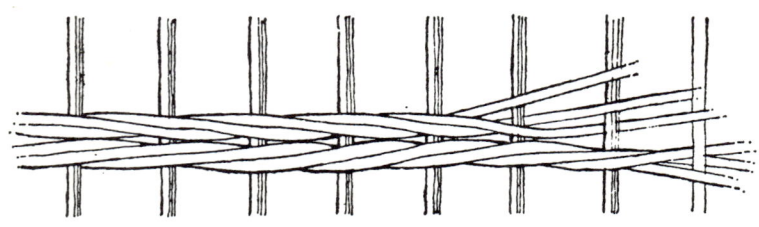

FIG. 44

Chain *Wale* (44) consists of two rounds, one of waling and one of reversed waling. Reversed waling is worked the same as ordinary waling except that each weaver passes under the others instead of over them.

Double *Chain* *Wale* is worked with pairs instead of single weavers, care being taken not to twist the weavers over each other.

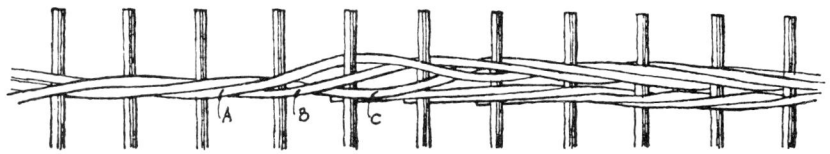

FIG. 45

Changing-the-Stroke (45) from the first round to the second, in a Chain-wale. This is not difficult if one remembers that CBA belong to the first round and so are not reversed. The second A is reversed and others thereafter.

The reverse round of a chain-wale is completed by taking the weavers to the inside so that they come together with those of the first round and complete the movement.

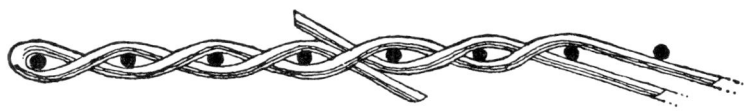

FIG. 46

Pairing (46) is usually begun by doubling a weaver round a stake. The join is shown.

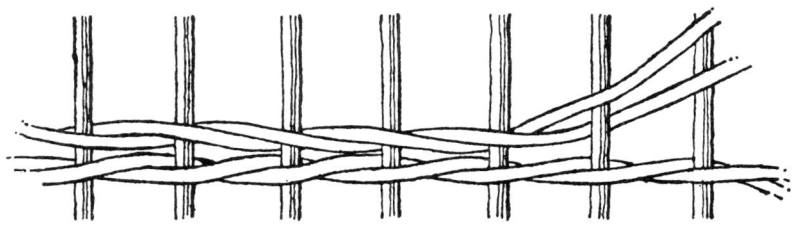

FIG. 47

Chain Pairing (47). Like Chain Waling (44), it consists of one round of pairing followed by one of reverse pairing, when the weavers are taken under and over each other instead of over and under.

TECHNIQUE

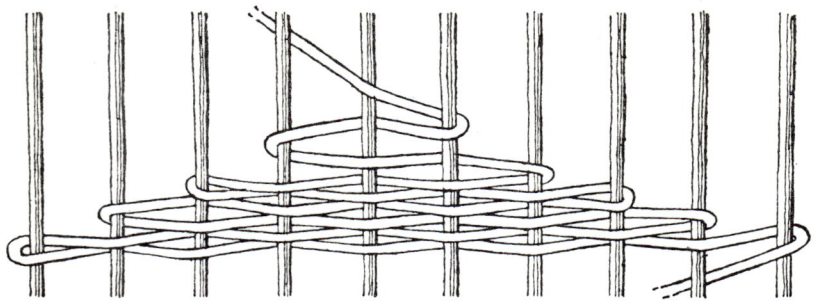

FIG. 48

Packing (48) builds up any part of a basket or base by a change in the normal line of the weaving, with one' or more short turns.

Decorative Weaves

When dyed cane is used (see APPENDIX A, page 139) the following decorative weaves may be worked.

Pairing. One plain and one coloured weaver over an even number of stakes produces stripes. One plain and one coloured weaver over an uneven number of stakes produces a spiral.

3-rod Waling

(A) With three weavers of different colours worked over a number of stakes divisible by the number of weavers (3), each colour will produce a vertical stripe.

(B) When the number of stakes is divisible by the number of weavers plus one, one coloured and two natural weavers will produce a variegated effect outside and a spiral inside the basket.

(C) When the number of stakes is divisible by the number of weavers plus two, the spiral will be outside (going to the right) and the variegation inside.

(D) To reverse the spiral at C and make it go to the left, cut off all three weavers, and reinsert them and wale from right to left. The coloured weaver comes out of a space where there is already a coloured one.

(E) A spiral of coloured dots is made with one coloured and two natural weavers and the stakes divisible by three. Work three rounds of wale, then let the coloured weaver and a natural one change places and work three rounds. Continue these six rounds.

N.B. The change-of-stroke would not be used in these decorative wales.

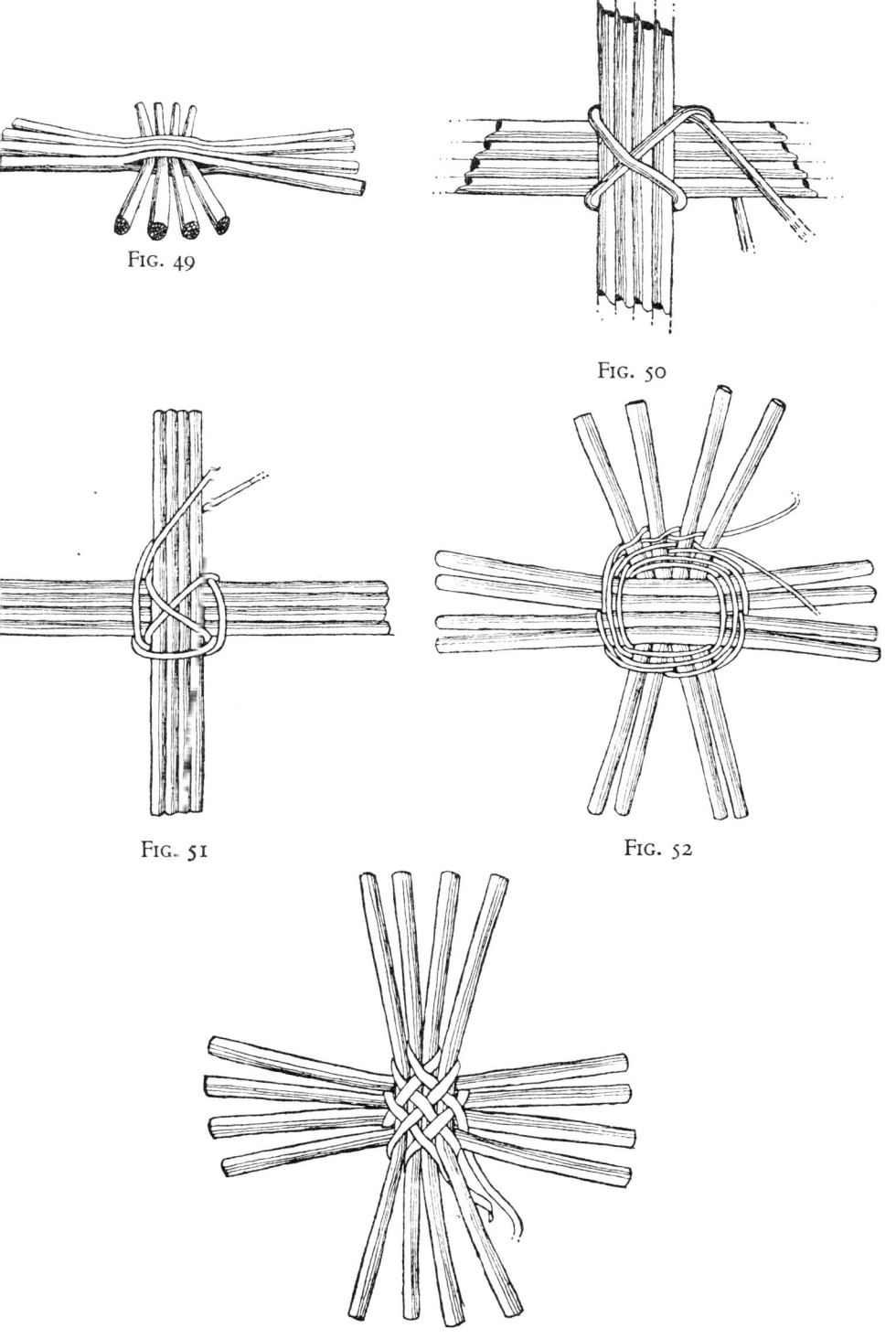

Fig. 49

Fig. 50

Fig. 51

Fig. 52

Fig. 53

41

TECHNIQUE

Bases

Round Base (49). A given number of sticks are pierced at their centres with knife or bodkin and others are put through them. If an uneven number is used, the greater goes through the lesser. These interwoven sticks are called a *Slath*.

A decorative beginning to the tying of the slath (50). A single weaver is bent at the centre.

Tying the slath with pairing (51). This is usually done twice or three times round.

Opening out (52). After the slath had been tied in its four parts these are divided, in the case of 4 through 4 first in twos for one round of pairing and then singly, opening the sticks out like a wheel. The base is then paired until the right size. (No decorative cross has been made as in Fig. 50.)

Another decoration of the slath worked with lapping, chair cane or willow skein (53). Begin with a large cross as shown in Fig. 50. Work with both ends until the interlacing looks like the diagram. It is not necessary to make diagonal crossings at the back, and the two canes will come out next to each other. Finish by tying the blocks of 4 with one round of pairing.

For a *Randed* base (54) an extra short stick will be needed to make an odd number. After the slath is tied in blocks of 4 with one or two lines of pairing, the end of the short stick is slyped and put into the cut as shown. One end of the pairing weaver is then dropped and the other is used to rand the slath open. The weaving cane in this case is not doubled but bent a few inches from one end.

If the bottom sticks are of fine material, do not pierce them but just lay them across each other. This shows a *base where sticks and weaver are the same thickness* and which will either be randed or needs an odd number of sticks (55). The unshaded stick X is the

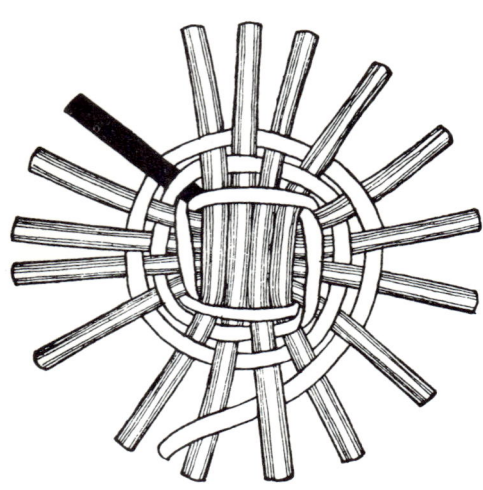

FIG. 54

TECHNIQUE

end of the weaver which is looped over to make the extra stick. This is a convenient beginning to a round basket where sticks and stakes are cut in one.

An Oval Base. The short sticks are pierced with a knife or bodkin and the long ones put through them The slath is then tied with a round or flat weaver, the short end being put down the slit in two canes at one end and the cross made. From this proceed to wind, crossing each stick at the back and making a cross at the other end. Here

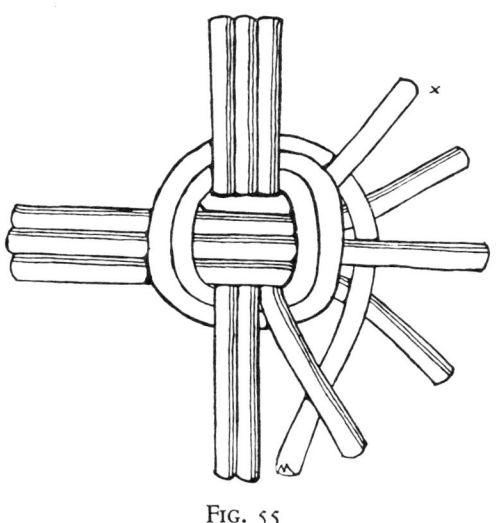

FIG. 55

add another weaver and pair the slath twice round. Then open out the ends. This may be done by pairing or by randing with two canes, as shown in the drawing (56) The whole base may be paired or randed but a paired base has an inherent tendency to twist, overcome in part by reverse or fitch pairing. *A randed base will not twist.*

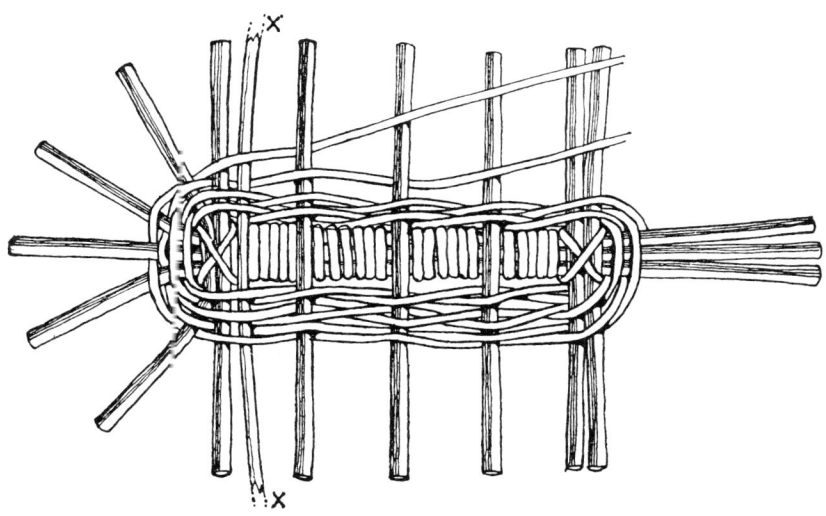

FIG. 56

43

TECHNIQUE

The stake X in the drawing is *not essential* to an oval basket. It is a *league*, that is: a stake which passes right round the basket, taking the weight. To cut a league make it the same thickness as the stakes and twice the length of

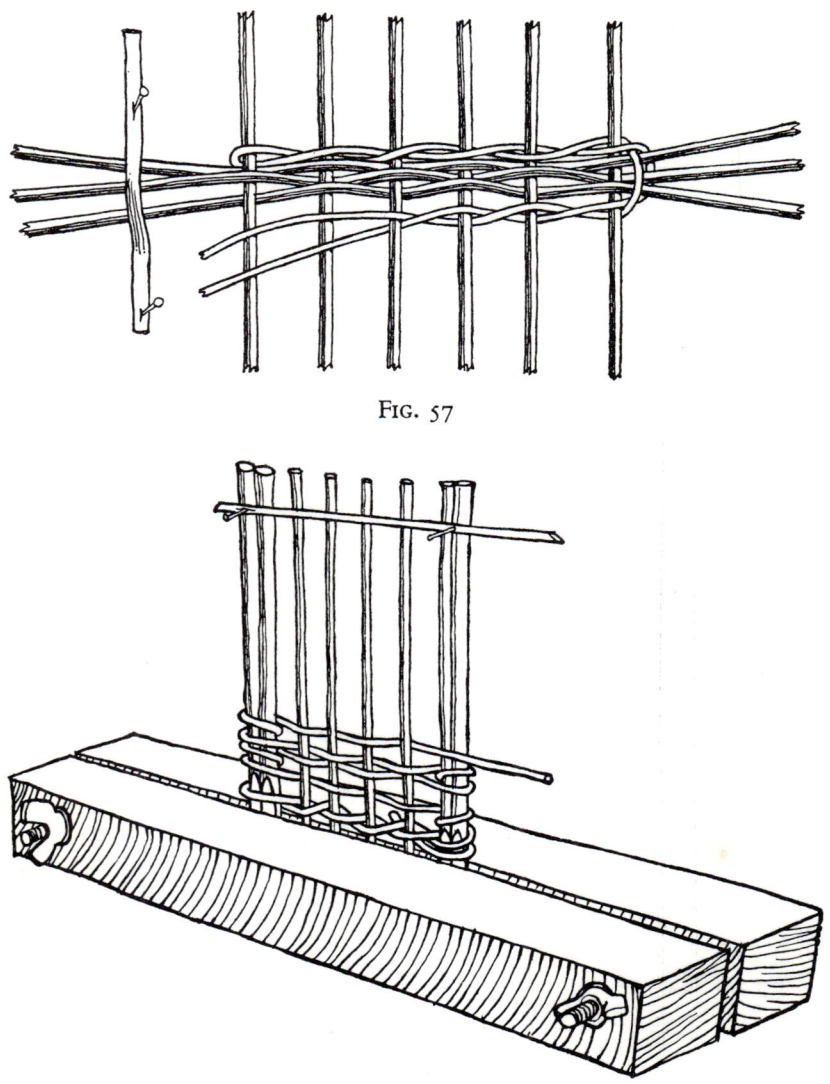

Fig. 57

Fig. 58

TECHNIQUE

the stakes plus the width of the base. It may be put through the base after weaving, using a bodkin, but is easier if added after the first round of opening out. Two leagues are usually used. It is worked into the upsetting at either side exactly like a stake.

An Oval Base where sticks are not pierced but interwoven (57). It is used when sticks and stakes are cut in one. The flat piece nailed down helps to hold the stakes while interlacing. Extra stakes will be added at the ends as the work proceeds. After the initial pairing the base may be randed. A single cane may be used if a short stick is added to make the odd number.

A Rectangular Base is made in a screw-block (58). The four outside sticks are of thick material and are slyped at both sides to go into the block. The first and last rows of the base are paired. The rest is randed, with round turns taken between to keep the work level.

A Base or Lid on a Shaped Frame (59). The sticks are scallomed, that is: thinned down to a long, flat point and taken round the frame as shown. The randed weave begins at the centre and is worked the same way as in the rectangular base. When about 1½ ins. away from the other end the ends of the sticks are scallomed as before and the weaving finished. Scalloming is easier to work with willow than with cane because the rods kink and stay rigid when dry. The cutting of a right-angled corner is shown in the small drawing.

A Shaping Board (60) is an aid to making a frame. The willow rod or heavy cane is tied to it when damp and

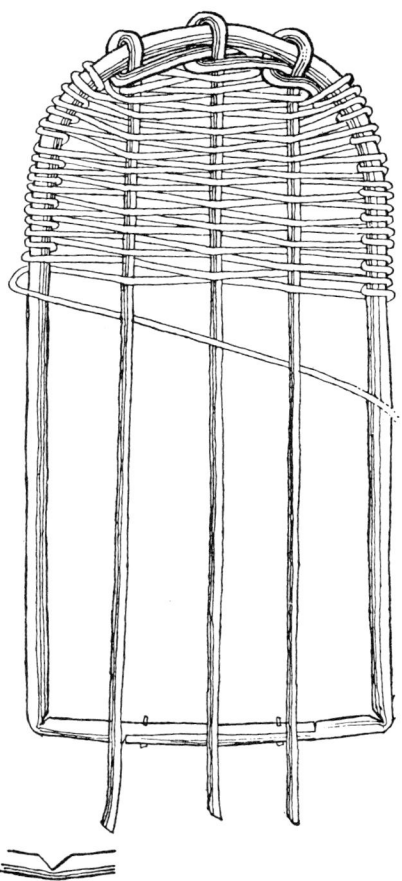

FIG. 59

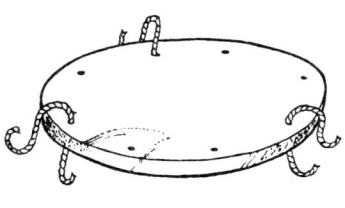

FIG. 60

45

TECHNIQUE

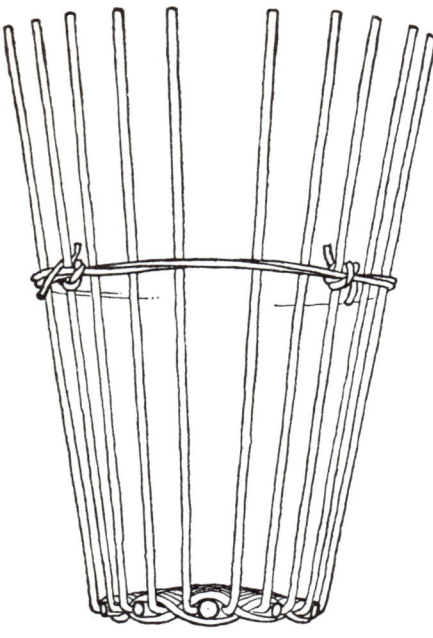

FIG. 61

allowed to dry. The slyped overlap, as shown in Fig. 59, is lightly nailed to the edge of the board. Any shape of frame may be made in this way, but the board should be slightly smaller than the finished base.

The professional worker will not need such an aid but it will be helpful to the amateur in making an exact shape.

·For the use of a *Wooden Base* with holes, see *Foot Border*, page 57, Fig. 92.

Insertion of Stakes (61) in a simple round or oval base, usually one on either side of the bottom sticks, which are first cut off closely. The stakes are then pricked up (see VOCABULARY, page 136), and held together with a twisted hoop until the upsett is put on.

Upsetting is the most important part of any basket and determines the final shape. The first round is worked on the bottom to cover up the angles of the bent stakes and the ends of the bottom sticks and to give the basket a firm rim to stand on. It

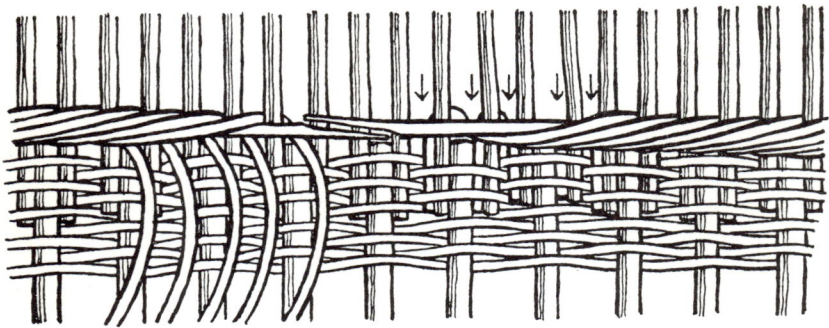

FIG. 62

TECHNIQUE

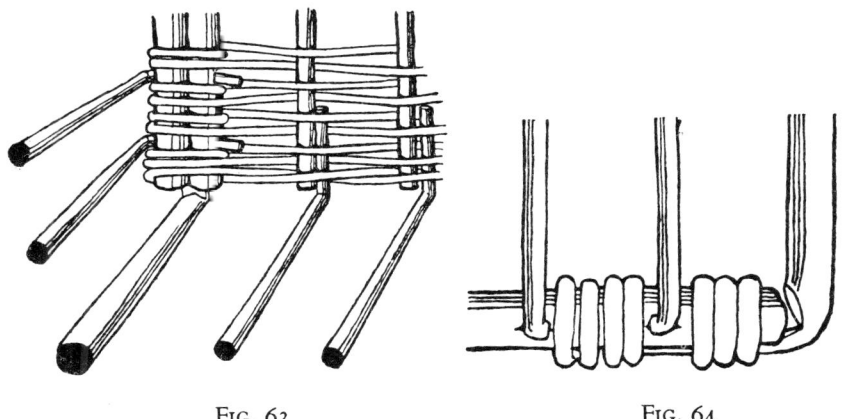

FIG. 63   FIG. 64

may be a 4-, 5- or 6-rod wale. Fig. 62 shows a 5-rod wale worked over a core of a slightly thicker cane which is slyped at both ends so that they will lie together. When worked on an oval base it is best to start the wale at one end so that the core joins on the curve.

The start of an upsett must be very firm. In canework the weavers should be put down into the base on the left-hand side of consecutive stakes and brought round behind them to the right. (The bottom is facing the worker.) They will then be tightly locked. This is shown by arrows in Fig. 62. After the first round the base is set up on the table or workboard and the subsequent rounds of upsetting are worked bringing the stakes into the right position. (See DESIGN, page 85.)

Stakes into a Rectangular Woven or Frame Base. Fig. 63 shows the detail of a corner post which has been slyped and the point put down by the end cane inside the weaving. A bodkin is driven at intervals into the side sticks of the base at a slight upward angle to make holes for slyped stakes (64).

Borders

A simple *Scallop* (65). The length of standing stakes required depends on the distance between them and can easily be measured with an odd piece. The ends should go well down into the weave.

A *Scallop* (66, 67), where A goes behind B, over C and D and down by the left of E. For length of standing stakes see last border.

A simple *Trac* border (68) requires only a couple of inches of standing stake.

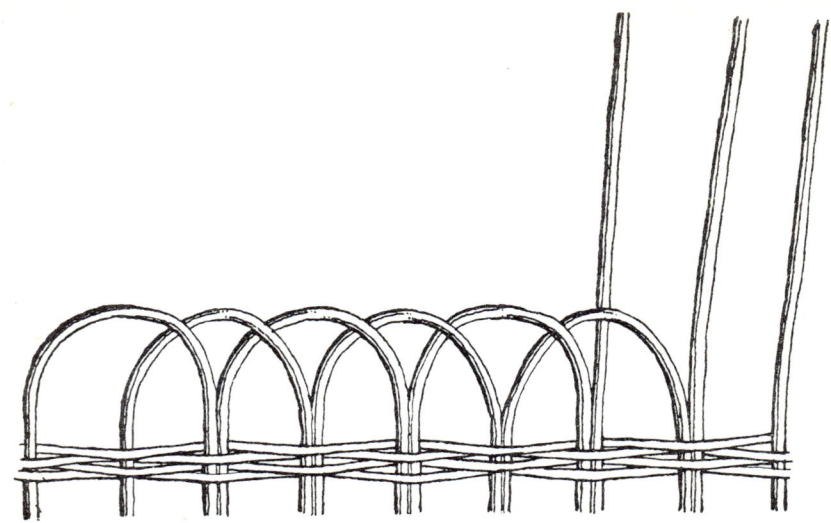

Fig. 65

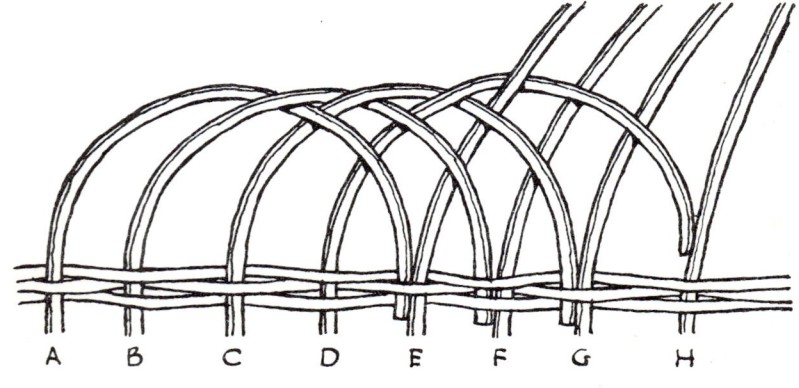

Fig. 66

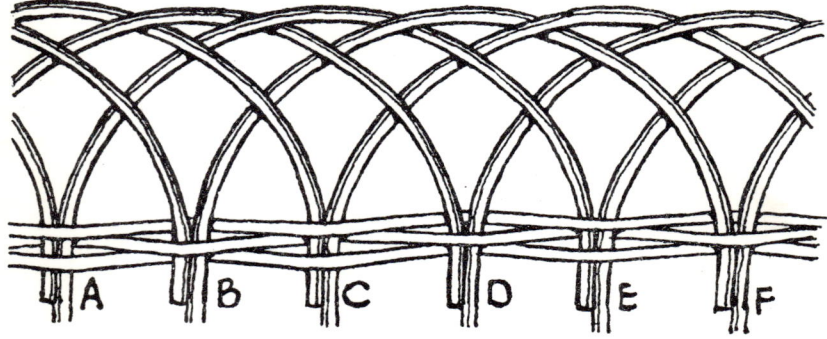

Fig. 67

TECHNIQUE

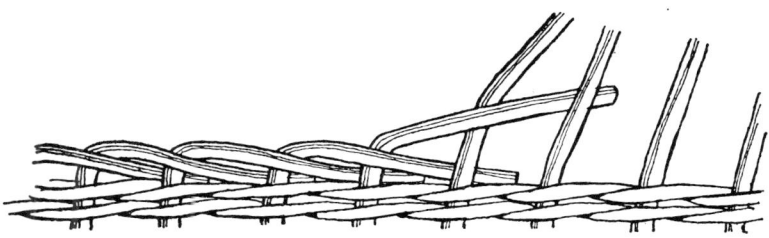

FIG. 68

A Trac border worked with pairs of stakes (69). In front of 1, behind 1, in front of 1, behind 1. To work this type of border hold each pair of canes at the bend with the finger and thumb of the left hand and bring them down with the right hand. This border should be tight and upright. When worked in willow the finish requires great care. The rods should be slightly twisted to stop them from cracking. Length of standing stake is about 6 ins. if stakes are 1 in. apart.

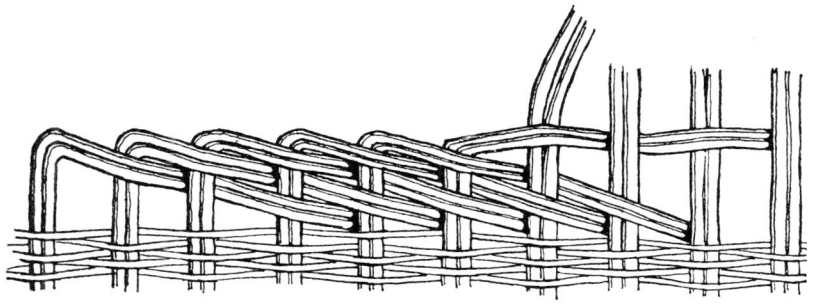

FIG. 69

A composite Trac border worked in 3 movements (70). (Cane.)
  i. Take each stake behind 1, in front of 1, behind 1, and in front. All stakes now lie on the front of the work.
  ii. Take each stake behind the next all the way round. Stakes will now be pointing upwards to the right.
  iii. Take each stake behind the next all round. Stakes will now point down and to the right. Length of standing stake is about 9 ins. when stakes are 1 in. apart.

The border looks well worked in pairs and has the advantage of having the ends hidden.

49

TECHNIQUE

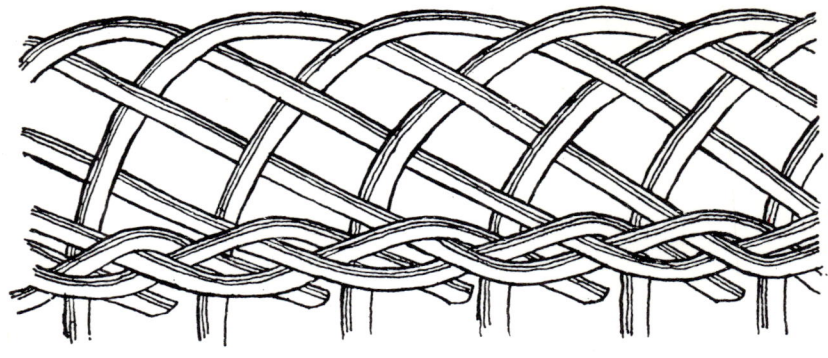

FIG. 70

There are many *tracs*. These are only three. Length of standing stakes will vary according to the distance they travel.

An excellent *Roll Border* for tray or basket may be made by working three or more rounds of a trac of over 2, after the first round of behind 2 to bring the stakes down to a horizontal position. The standing stakes for this should be 11 ins. or 12 ins. long on a tray; longer if a wider roll is required.

The 3-rod Plain Border (71–74)

71. Take 1 behind 2, 2 behind 3, 3 behind 4.

72. Take 1 in front of 3 and 4, behind 5 and to the front between 5 and 6. Take 4 down with and behind it.

73. Take 2 in front of 4 and 5, behind 6 and to the front between 6 and 7. Take 5 down with and behind it. Do the same movement with 3 and 4. Continue, always taking the front cane of the left-hand pair. Short ends will be left to be cut off.

74. The finish of the border *in cane*. After the last upright stake and its fellow have been brought down and put round and under stake 1, three pairs of stakes will be pointing to the right, and the longer ones should be called ABC. Thread them through one by one as shown, thus completing the pattern. It will be seen that they always pass *in front* of the stakes 2, 3 and 4. Help them through with the bodkin. When a willow basket is to have a lid, it is usual to cram down A, B and C instead of working them through. They are kinked at right angles at a point just to the left of the next stake, and slyped for about 1 in. below the kink. This short slyped end is inserted into the basket to the left and beside the stake and tapped down with the rapping iron. Length of standing stake when stakes are $\frac{5}{8}$ in. apart, as on a wooden tray base, 5 ins., but when 1 in. apart, 9 ins.

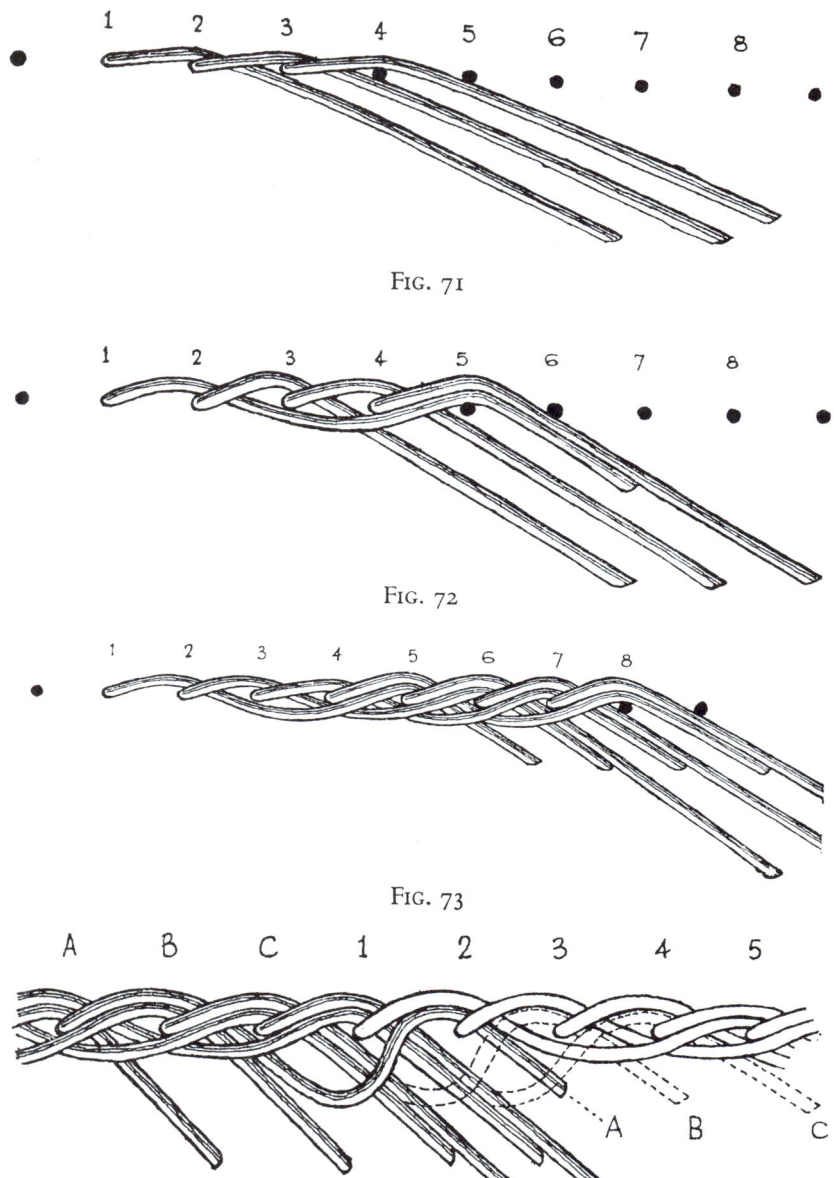

FIG. 71

FIG. 72

FIG. 73

FIG. 74
THE 3-ROD PLAIN BORDER

TECHNIQUE

FIG. 75

A 3-rod Plain Border with a Follow-on Trac (75). A cane border. After the last border has been completed the ends should be 3–4 ins. long; slype them and pass each one under the next two and through to the inside between the border and the weaving, so that it rests against the third upright to the right. Standing stake length = 2 ins. or 3 ins. longer than for the 3-rod border alone.

FIG. 76

A 3-rod Plain Border with a Back-Trac (76). The Back-Trac is worked after the border in Figs. 71–74 has been completed. The ends are pointing outwards and to the right. The Back-Trac is worked on the far side of the basket and goes from right to left. Each stake goes over the next two and under the third. Pull tight. Standing stake length = 4 ins. or 5 ins. longer than for the 3-rod plain border.

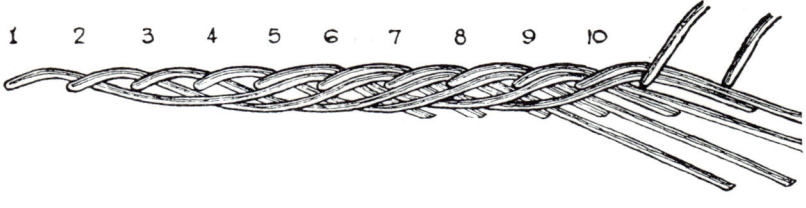

FIG. 77

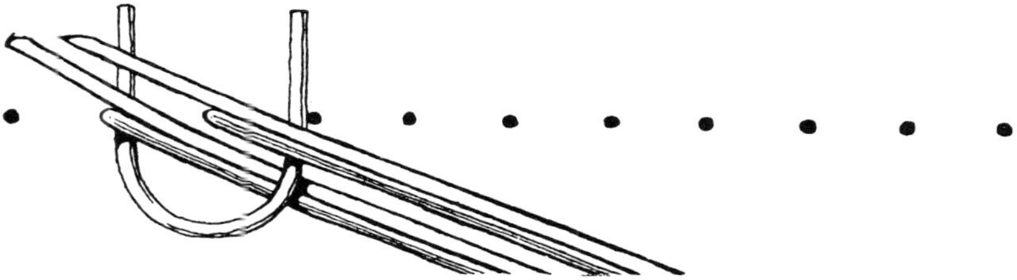

TECHNIQUE

Fig. 78

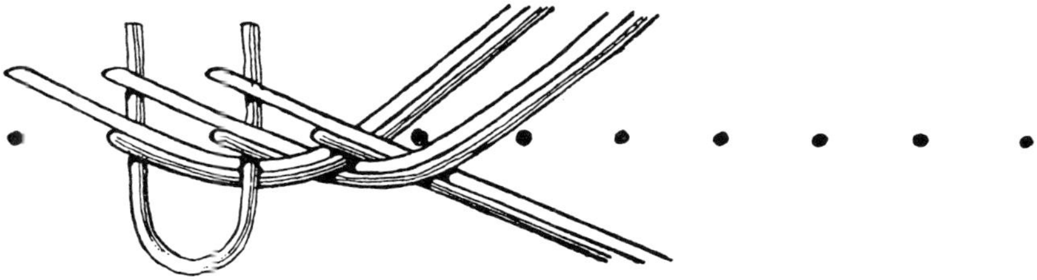

Fig. 79

Fig. 80

Fig. 81

THREE-PAIR PLAIT (FIGS. 78–83)

TECHNIQUE

Fig. 82

Fig. 83
THREE-PAIR PLAIT (*continued*)

A 4-rod Plain Border (77). This is worked the same way as the 3-rod plain border in Figs. 71–74 but the first, second, third and fourth canes are brought down and the first cane passes in front of the fifth and behind the sixth. The fifth cane is brought down with it. It needs about 12 ins. of standing stake when stakes are 1 in. apart.

3-pair Plait (78–83). Standing stake length above the weaving when stakes are $\frac{5}{8}$ in. apart, as on a wooden tray base = 6 ins. Three extra stakes 6 ins. long are required the same thickness as the stakes and a "guide" stick about 4 ins. long. The "guide" is shown as a hairpin shape and the extra stakes unshaded.

Fig. 82 shows the finish of the border. The last two pairs are taken up and through where the "guide" now is and the "guide" removed. The first pair has been completed in the drawing. The last two extra stakes are in position and the long stakes have only to be brought down and through.

N.B. Many caneworkers do not use the extra stakes at all and it is perfectly possible to work the border without them, but they are essential in willow work. Fig. 83 shows how the extra canes may be removed and the pairs taken through in their places. This has been done with the first pair. The last two extra stakes are shown black and the second is in the process of being removed.

TECHNIQUE

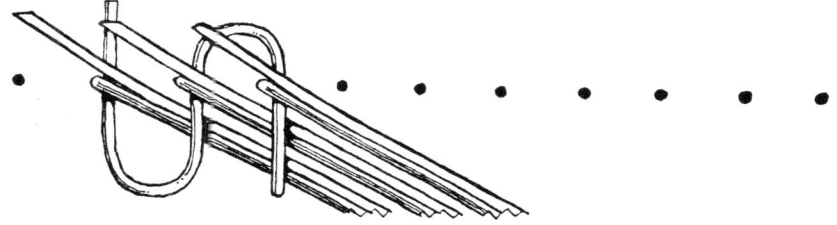

FIG. 84

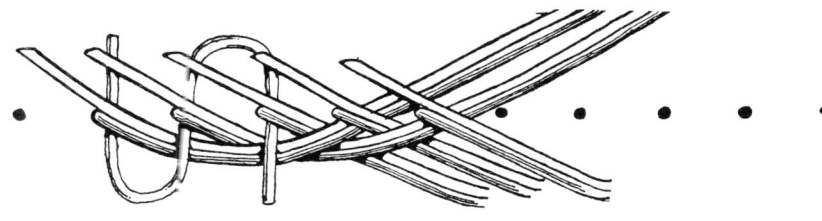

FIG. 85

FIG. 86

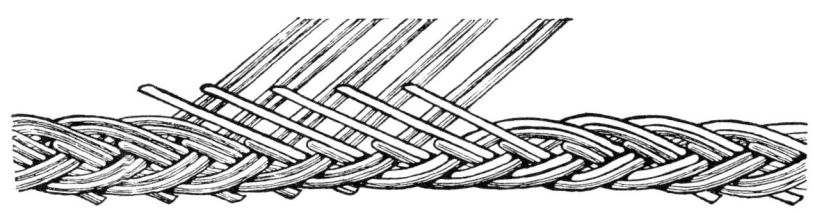

FIG. 87
FIVE-PAIR PLAIT (FIGS. 84–89)

TECHNIQUE

Fig. 88

Fig. 89

FIVE-PAIR PLAIT (*continued*)

5-*pair Plait* (84–89). Standing stakes length when stakes are $\frac{5}{8}$ in. apart is 9 ins., but a large plait on a shopping basket may take double this length or more. Five extra stakes 9 ins. long are needed and a "guide" 7 ins. or 8 ins. long, longer if the plait is larger.

See 3-*pair Plait* (Page 54) for the method. Fig. 89 gives the alternative finish.

If *a plait* is to be worked *on the side* of a basket, the standing stakes should be 2 or 3 ins. longer, and are squeezed or pricked and brought down behind 2 all the way round. They will then be at right angles to the basket and the plait is worked with the basket held on its side.

A 4-*pair Plait* is worked like the other two but with four extra stakes. It begins as in Fig. 84 and continues as in Fig. 85, except that instead of laying in the fifth extra the first pair are brought down to make the first threedown. The border proceeds with three working pairs at the bottom and one at the top.

A *Madeira-Type Border*. Needs 9 ins. of standing stake when the triple stakes have $\frac{5}{8}$ in. between them.

90. The threes are taken down behind two threes all the way round.

56

TECHNIQUE

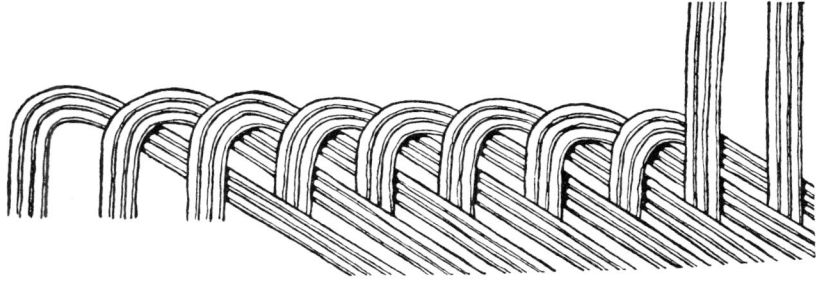

FIG. 90

FIG. 91

91. The threes are taken over two and through to the back. They are then taken over one and brought to the front again underneath and cut off.
This border is effective if worked in three colours. Two coloured stakes can be added to a natural stake when the basket is ready to border and will not show if a deep band of 4-rod waling (Fig. 43) has been worked before the border. This will hide the additional ends on both sides of the basket. It is seldom worked in willow but used to be in wicker chairs.

A Foot-Border. (92) This is a trac border used for securing stakes to a wooden base with holes in it. The movement is behind 1, in front of 2, behind 1, and takes about 3 ins. of stake. Other tracs may also be used.

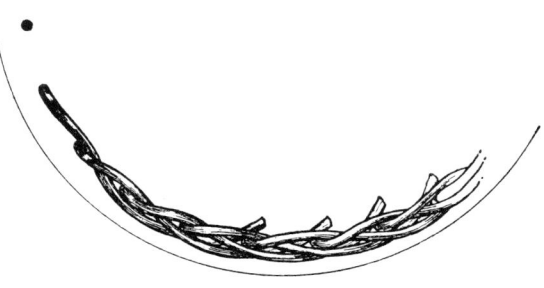

FIG. 92

TECHNIQUE

Handles

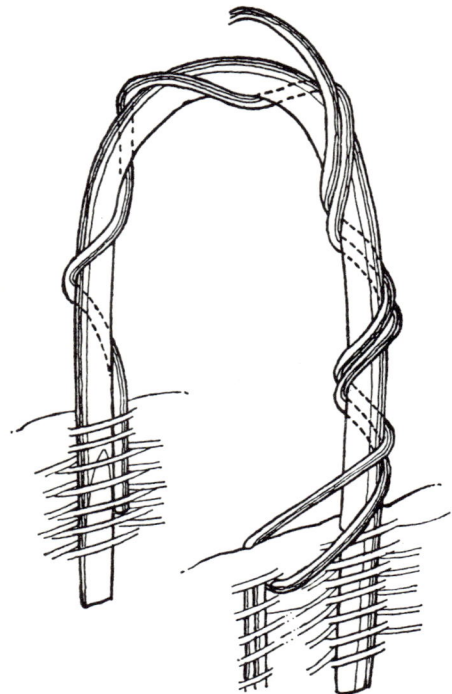

FIG. 93

ROPED HANDLE. *Cane Basketry*. The average number of turns round the bow of a shopping basket is five (93). It may be less on a shorter handle. The lapping cane should be as long as possible, but if a second has to be used, the end of the first piece is woven away into the wale, and the second is introduced in the same way and carries on the movement. The first loop through the basket is held well over to the stake to the left of the bow, so that subsequent ones lie to the right of it and fill the space between it and the bow (94).

In *willow* work use three or four rods, each of which will twist across and come back again once. They start alternatively at each side, either singly, in pairs or even threes. The rods are very mellow and are twisted themselves before being used. To finish, each set of rods is either put into the wale or brought up, tied once round the handle and cut off.

On a lid do the same as for the cane type, inserting the

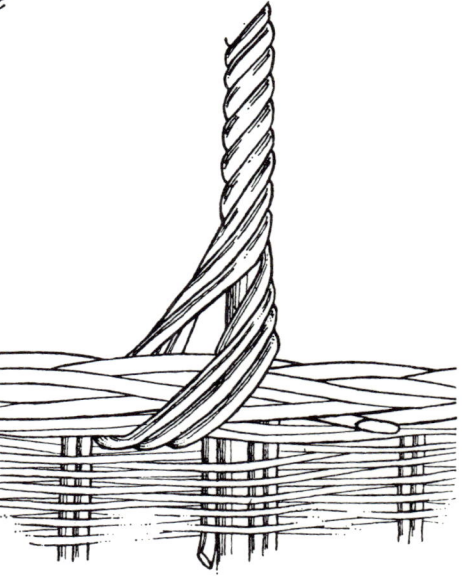

FIG. 94

TECHNIQUE

bow or bows during weaving, and taking the wrapping cane down into the weaving in front and to the left of the bow, but bringing it out again at the left, a couple of rows of weaving further back. In subsequent turns-round the cane goes down to the right of the last one and comes up again behind the last one.

LAPPED HANDLE in cane or willow skein with interweaving (95). This is not so strong as a roped handle and the cross-over is more for ornament than strength. Bows should always be pegged. *Pegging* with a short peg is done by driving a bodkin through the bow from front to back, obliquely, below the wale. A slyped and scraped inch-long peg of No. 8 cane or willow is tapped through with iron or hammer. Ends are cut off. A long peg is 6 ins. or 8 ins. and has the ends woven into the wale.

Figs. 98 and 99 show other decorations used with the lapped method. Simple interweaving may be done with more than one cane and patterns and checks made.

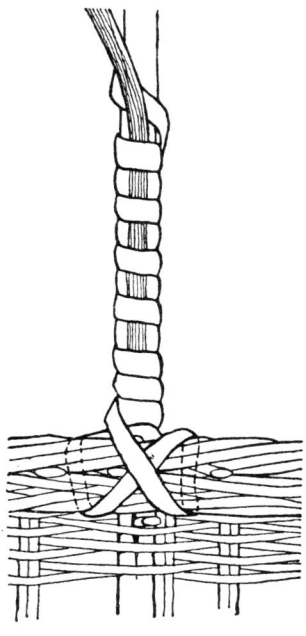

FIG. 95

Joining-in a new lapping cane or willow skein (96). The twist is tapped flat.

HERRINGBONE LISTING (97, 98)

Materials: A 2- or 3-bow handle nailed together at the top.
1 very long and 2 shorter lengths of lapping cane.
3 lengths of chair cane No. 6 or 4, 3½ times the length of the part of the bow to be listed.
1 length of No. 6 cane. (X in Fig. 97.)
2 lengths No. 8 cane (Y and Z).

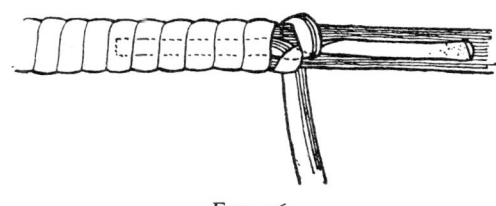

FIG. 96

Method: Lap one "leg" at each side, securing the ends to lie under the listed part. Lap a third "leg" to the join and work two rounds of twisting over the three bows, as shown in the drawing. Lay in X, Y and

59

TECHNIQUE

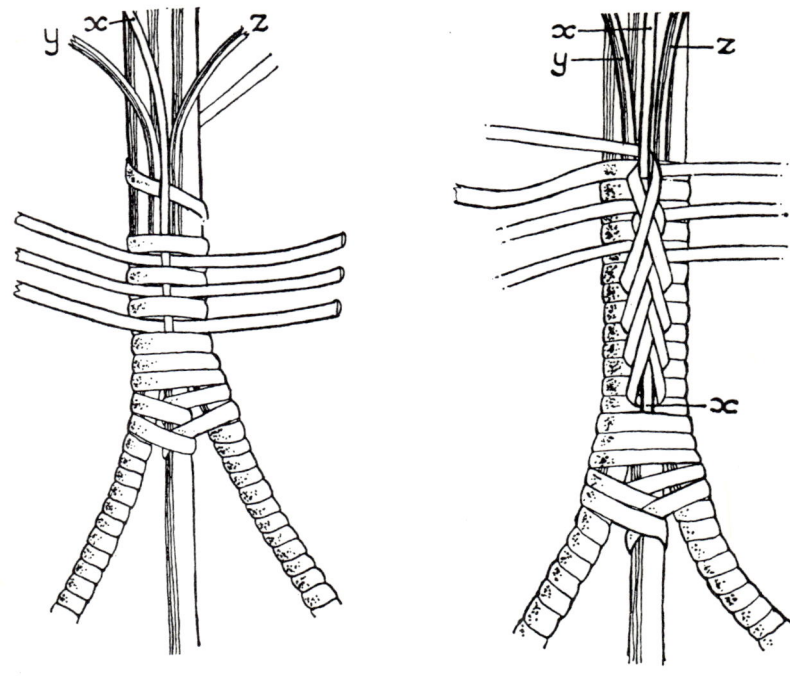

FIG. 97   FIG. 98

Z which simply lie in the grooves made by the joins of the three bows. Bind over all three or four times. Then bind in the three chair canes as shown in Fig. 97, wrong sides upwards, centres beneath X. Follow Fig. 98, taking the chair canes up, pair by pair, twisting them round X to lie out flat as before, and lapping once over X in between each.

To finish, judge the distance carefully, and hold the pairs forward after twisting instead of bringing them out at right angles, so that they are bound in with subsequent lapping. All ends are cut off so that they are hidden, and the last "leg" is finished. The central "legs" are not lapped.

Peg all three bows.

CROSSED LISTING (99)

Materials: A single bow.

1 long piece lapping cane.
1 long piece No. 4 chair cane.
1 piece No. 3 or 4 centre cane the length of the bow.

Method: Fig. 95 shows interweaving. Listing is worked over the interwoven No. 3 or 4 cane. Start by laying the centre of the length of chair cane under this, with the wrong side upwards. To finish bind the ends down under the last few laps.

DROP HANDLES (100). These may be fastened over the border or made first and fastened to the sides with a loop of flat cane or skein. Fig. 101 shows the mellow bow being bent round the bodkin. This may also be done by heating over the cane lamp, but practice is needed. To lap the handle, lay the right side of one end of the lapping cane or skein to the bow, pointing upwards, and turn the cane over it and round it and the bow. To finish: bind to the end, then allow the last three or four rounds to slacken, holding firmly above them. Turn the end and put it up between the slackened rounds and the bow with the right side to the bow. Tighten again with a screwing movement and pull the end up so that all is tight and cut it off close.

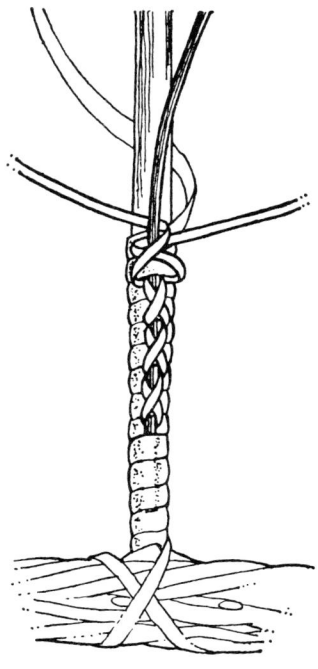

FIG. 99

Dropped Ring (102). Cane. Tie a length of a cane into a ring as in tying the first part of a reef or granny-knot, leaving one long and one short end. With the long end turn over the ring four times, returning to the start. Go round again letting these turns lie neatly beside the first ones. Cut off the ends and sew to the basket with a criss-cross of finer cane.

Turk's Head as a handle or button.

103. With a length of cane make two circles the size of the required ring or button with long end finishing at the top.

104. Cross the left-hand ring over the right-hand one (X) and put the long end to the left between them, over the right-hand and under the left-hand one.

105. Separate the two rings at the second cross (Y), which was made at the same time as X, and put the long end to the right between them.

106. Now turn the rings by taking hold of them with the right finger and thumb at the same place as they have been held until now. Turn the rings towards you until the last movement faces you and change hands again.

Cross the left-hand ring over the right-hand one and put the long end

TECHNIQUE

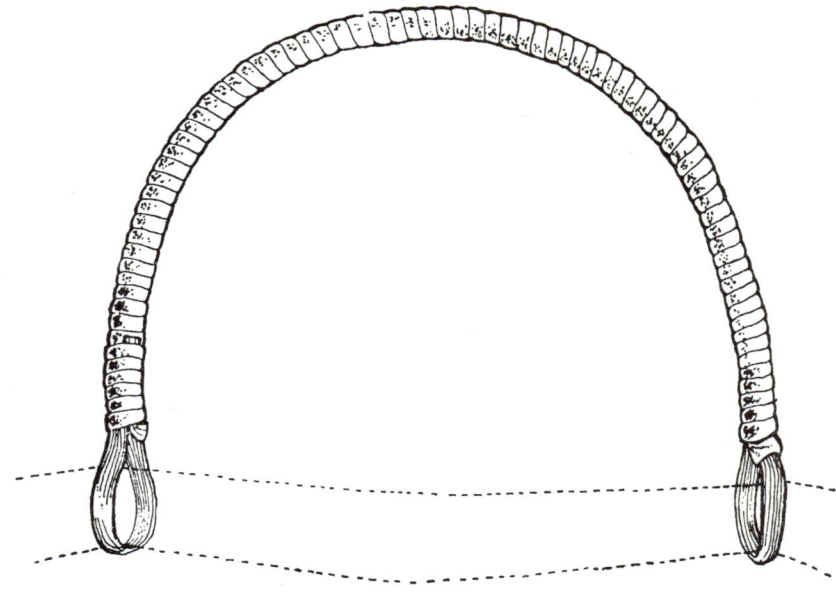

Fig. 100

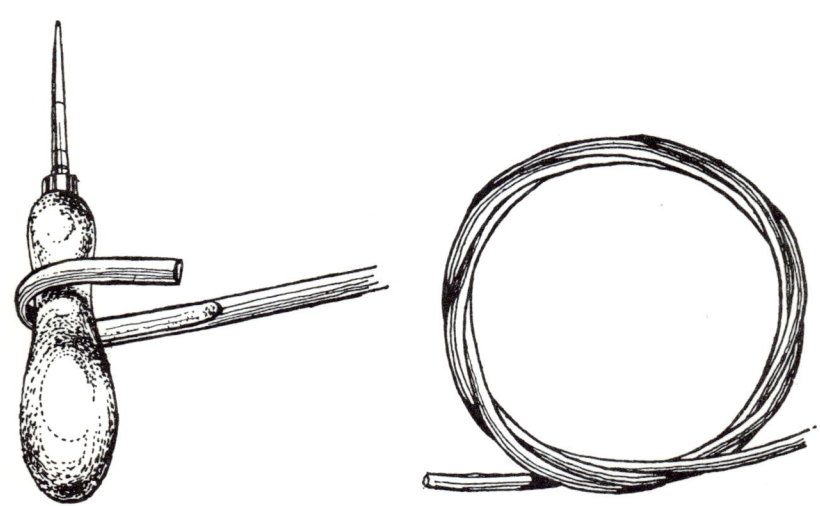

Fig. 101

Fig. 102

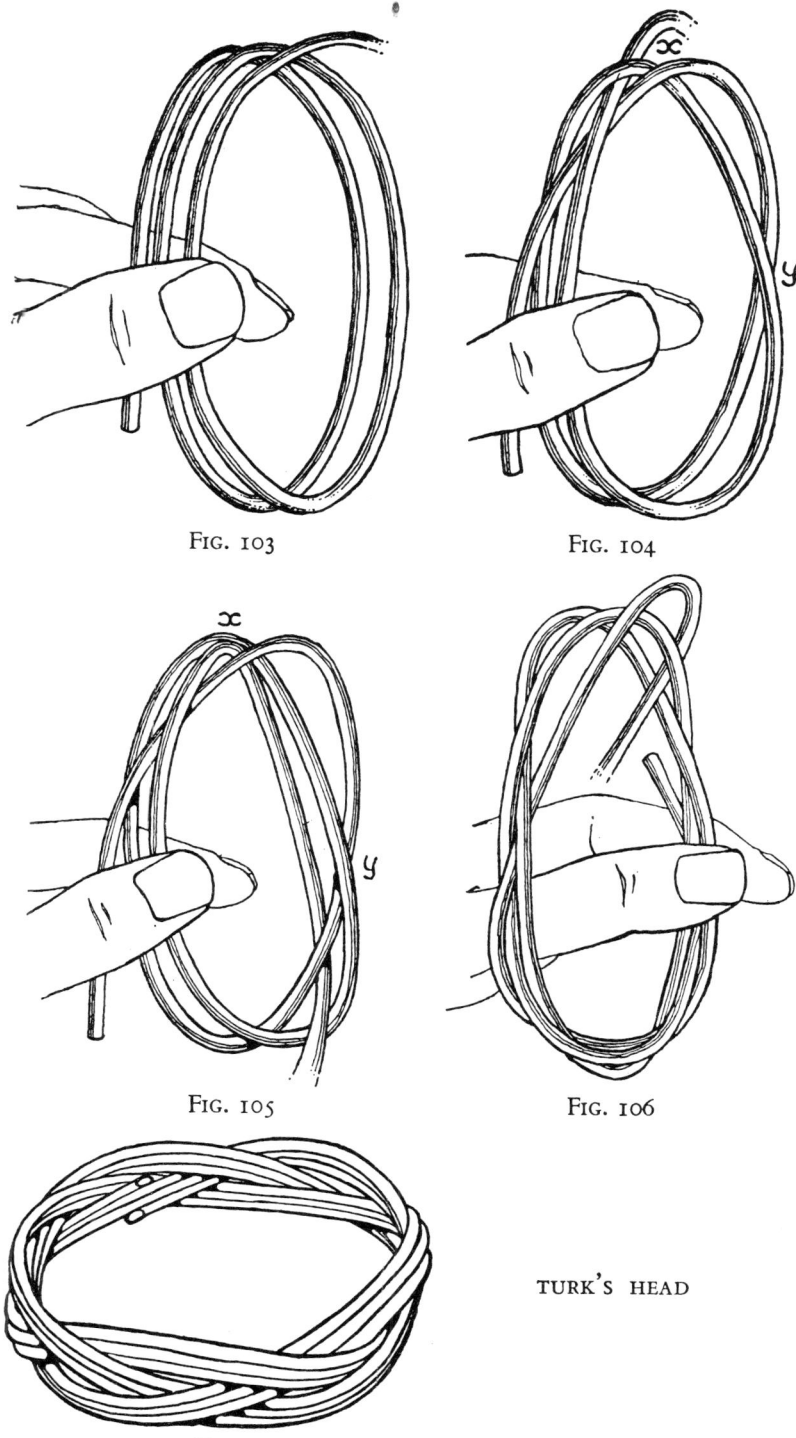

FIG. 103

FIG. 104

FIG. 105

FIG. 106

TURK'S HEAD

FIG. 107

TECHNIQUE

between them to the left, as in Fig. 104. Complete by putting the long end through and down by the short end.

N.B. The long end always goes over and down as in any plait.

107. The completed ring is doubled, trebled or quadrupled by simply following the short end round and round, always letting the new movement lie to the left of the old one.

This is the knot worked on a sailor's or scout's lanyard, and may be made of many sizes and used as a button or napkin ring, a drop handle or a trimming.

Bow Marks. When a handle-bow goes down into the fabric of the basket it is usual to make room for it by inserting a bow-mark by the side of the appropriate stake during the weaving, and working over it. This is a short piece of handle cane or willow the same size or a little smaller than the bow, slyped.

Where two or more bows will go in *together*, work two stakes as one with the bow-marks between them, beginning after the upsett.

Lids and Ledges

A ROUND LID is usually made on the same principle as a round base (Figs. 49 and 52). It may be woven in any way that agrees with the weave of its basket, but ribranding (Fig. 37) is particularly suitable.

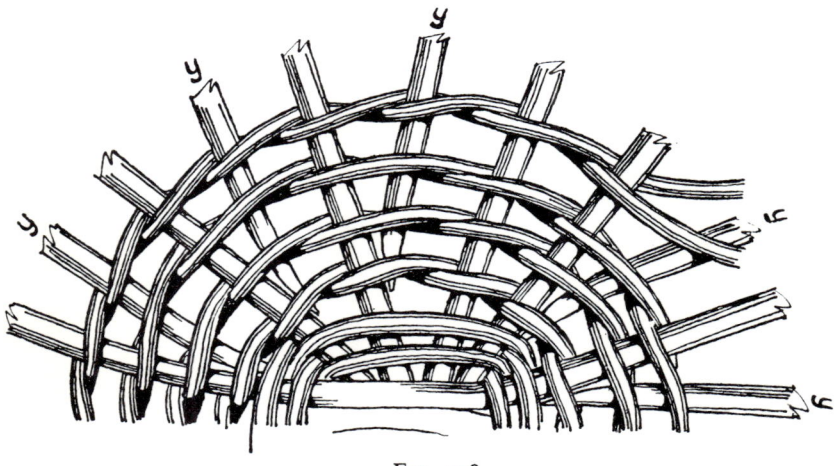

FIG. 108

TECHNIQUE

Sticks should be thicker than weavers. When a large lid is to be made add further sticks after opening out, as soon as the weaving will accommodate them. They are slyped and laid in as shown at Y in Fig. 108, then all are paired for one or two rounds before beginning any other weave.

The border on a lid may be worked with the sticks themselves or the sticks may be cut off and stakes inserted, one or two to each stick. With these a border is worked or, as in the case of Basket Recipe No. III, a *trunk cover*, when the stakes are upsett before bordering.

When a lid drops into a basket, a *ledge* must be worked into the basket. Fig. 109 shows a simple ledge, seen from inside the basket.

FIG. 109

Two rounds of 5-rod wale (see page 38) are worked on the inside of the basket, just below a trac border. Worked from the outside, five rods are used, each one going in front of one and behind four.

The ledge shown at Fig. 110 is worked with the bye-stakes or liners of a basket which should be cut about 3 ins. longer than normally. The border illustrated is the 3-rod plain with the follow-on trac and it was worked before the ledge. At a height of about 1 in. below the finished height the bye-stakes were squeezed and bent inwards; two rounds of waling were then worked over the stakes which were then bordered down. Two rounds of pairing were worked on the bye-stakes holding them at right angles to the basket, and then a simple trac border kept very tight. If this ledge is worked with a double trac border, the bye-stakes would be cut longer but

TECHNIQUE

would naturally not be bent inwards until after the border was completed. This ledge has the advantage of hiding the unsightly ends of a trac border.

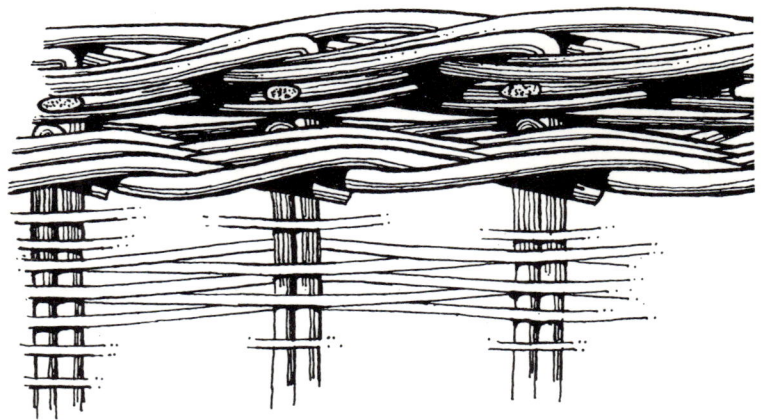

FIG. 110

A *ledge outside* a basket to hold a trunk cover generally consists of single round of 4- or 5-rod wale about 1 in. below the top of the basket, which is held in a little above it.

N.B. Cane workers will find a jam jar a great convenience in working ribranding on a lid. After pairing is completed, place the lid on the upturned jar and put the flat of the left hand on it allowing it to revolve, while weaving with the right hand.

Notches

To make the opening or notch in a wine-cradle or a dog basket first mark the outside stakes of the opening, A and B in Fig. 111. Then work a single round of 3-rod wale starting at the next stake to the right of B. When A is

FIG. 111

112   Garden Basket, Wales
      (see page 131)

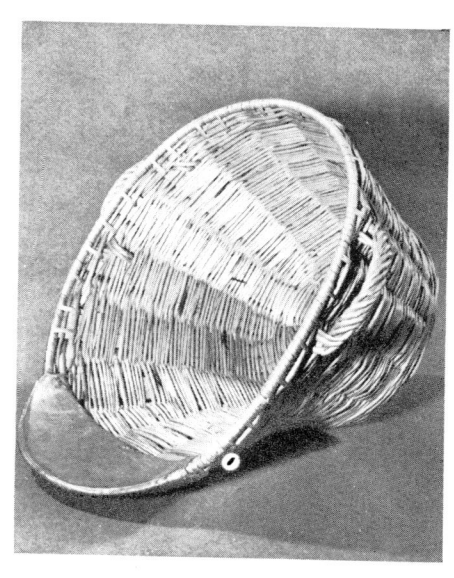

113   Malt Skip (see page 131)

114   Hack-Muck (see page 131)

115   Fruit Picker (see page 131)

116　Oval Shopper *(see page 131)*

TECHNIQUE

reached 1 and 2 stakes are brought down as in a 3-rod border and are used to complete the wale. More or less stakes may be brought down according to the size of notch required. The rods or canes for this round of 3-rod wale should be the same thickness as the stakes. Put in two stout corner posts at A and B.

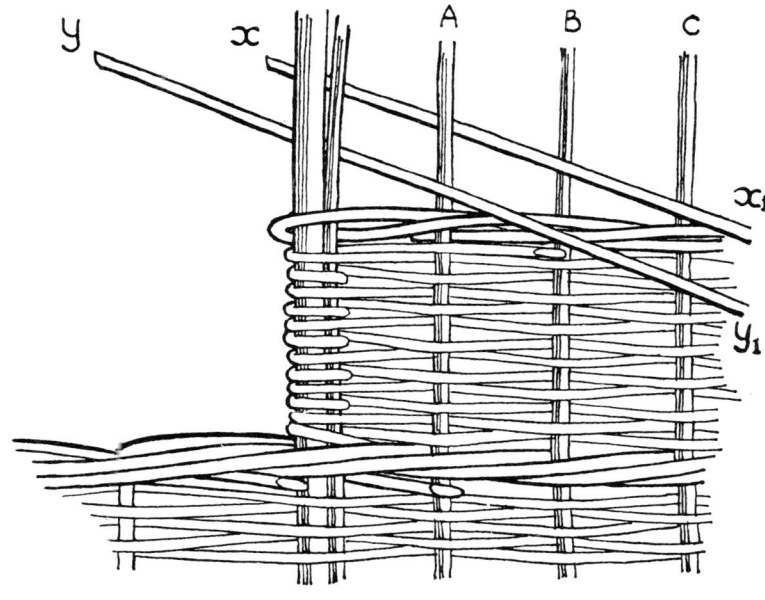

FIG. 117

After the basket has been worked to the desired height and the top wale put on, a 3-rod plain border is worked. Cut two rods X and Y (about 8 ins. long for a wine-cradle) the same size as the stakes and lay them in as shown at Fig. 117 with about half the length protruding beyond the post. Bring

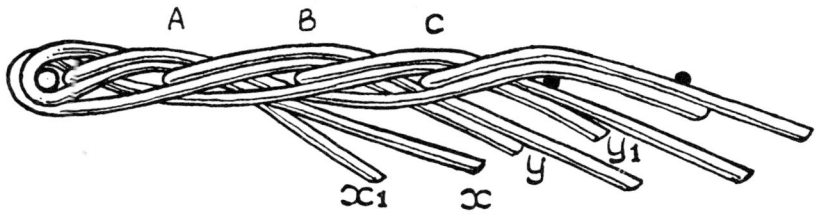

FIG. 118

TECHNIQUE

X round in front of the post and its stake, behind A, in front of B, and bring down the post-stake with it. Then bring Y round the post (below X), in front of A, behind B, in front of C, and bring A down with it. Take Y, 1, in front of B and behind C and bring B down with it. This gives the three pairs necessary to work the 3-rod plain border (73).

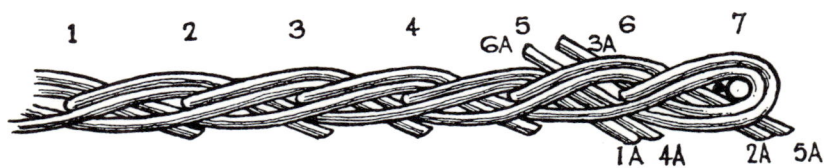

FIG. 119

Fig. 119 shows how the 3-rod plain border is completed at the left side of the notch. It will be seen that stake No. 7, by the left-hand corner post, is cut off before the border is worked.

The border is usually tied down at the posts in cane-work with an over-and-over of flat lapping such as chair cane. (See fig. 162).

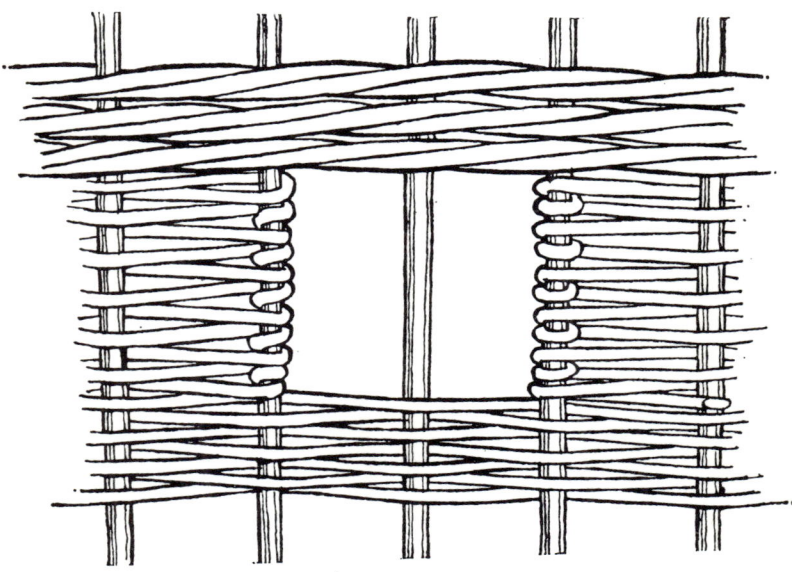

FIG. 120

TECHNIQUE

A *closed notch* (120) suitable as a strap-hole on a bicycle basket or finger-hole on a log basket. The central stake may be cut out after the border has been worked, leaving the ends protruding slightly, if a larger hole is needed.

Ties and Trimmings

The simplest fastening for a lid which rests on the edge of a basket is made of a single looped cane or willow, twisted, taken back into the weaving, tied and the ends threaded away (121). A smaller loop is made on the basket. A peg of handle cane or thick willow can secure this. Tying this peg to the basket may be done by cutting a neat groove round the peg to hold a string, or making a small hole in it with a red-hot nail, heated on a gas flame and held with pliers.

This *tie* or *noose* for a lid is used on fruit baskets and has the

FIG. 121

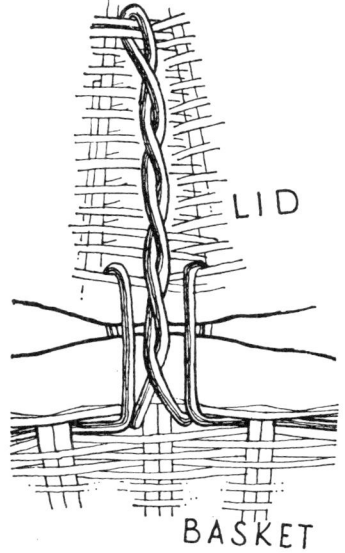

FIG. 122

advantage of holding the weaving of the lid (122). It may also be hinged with twists as in Fig. 121 going over the borders only.

A plait of three or five may be used instead of a twist. *A plait of five* (123) is not difficult and is strong enough for small handles also. Two long pieces of fine cane or willow and one half the length

71

TECHNIQUE

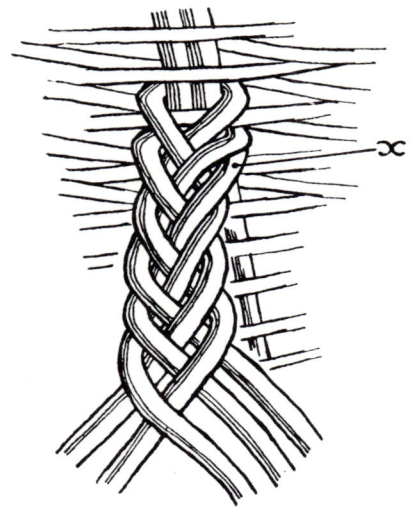

FIG. 123

marked X are required. The first two are looped round a stake, one below the other and X goes in singly. The movement of the plait is that the outside canes always come across over two canes. In a three-plait they come across over one cane.

Construction of a Round Frame Basket

This type of basket is made quite differently from any other. At its simplest it is still made by gypsies and is known in France as a *pannier rustique*, a rustic basket. At its most complicated it takes forms like the Ose (132), the shoe basket (134), the Arbroath fish baskets (5), the scull (6), the Yarmouth herring swill (10) and the potato basket (13). As the experts say, in all its forms it is made by hand and eye, not by measurement, and if the first rings are wrong then it will never come right.

Fig. 128 shows *the two rings* of a round shopping basket fastened temporarily together. The slyped and nailed joins are permanent, one at the bottom and one at the side. The best material for these rings is rigid: hazel, ash or willow. If centre handle cane or kubu has to be used the basket must be made with *a frame* to hold the rings to shape. This may be *a cross* of wood with its four ends nailed temporarily to the horizontal ring. Two ends will be nailed

124 Egg Basket
(see page 131)

125 Cat Basket
(see page 131)

126 Bottle Basket
(see page 131)

127 Log Basket (see page 132)

at the junctions of the two rings. The pieces of the crossframe will each measure the inner diameter of the horizontal ring. Without a frame the horizontal ring will pull down in weaving.

If the handle ring passes outside the horizontal ring, as in Fig. 128, it must be a little larger or the basket will be slightly melon-shaped.

The cross-frame is nailed in after the rings have been tied together.

N.B. This is not a type of basket for a beginner. It gives scope for design and shape but the maker must be prepared to make two or three before getting the shape perfect and every size and shape may need its own frame. It is most satisfactory when made and woven with rigid or semi-rigid materials. Willow-skein or split or round palembang are better for weaving than lapping or centre cane. The latter is frequently used, particularly for rectangular forms, but is seldom wholly satisfactory from a design viewpoint. (See Fig. 146.)

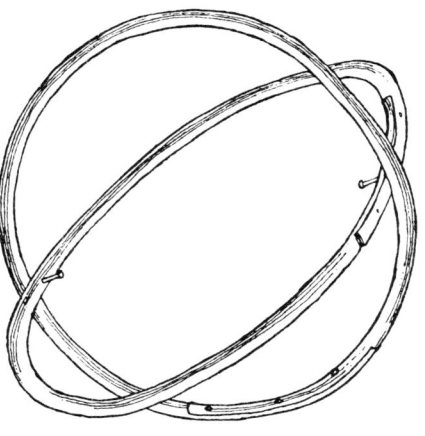

FIG. 128

The placing of the stakes and actual *frame construction* (129). The stakes are cut in pairs and go in during the actual weaving. It will be seen that A, B and C go in very early, though there is no rule and every shape varies.

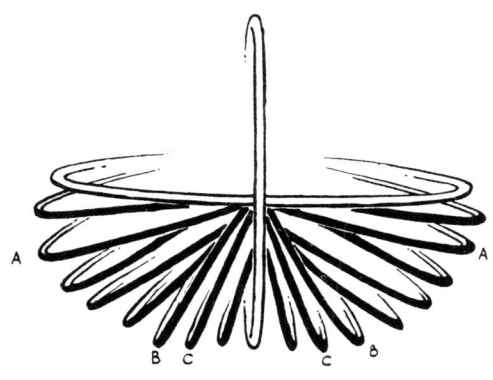

FIG. 129

One method of tying the two circles together using flat material (130).

The completed tie (131) which has been carried over to lap the handle. When one side has been tied then the other is tied also, giving a hold for the first stakes to go in. These are woven in as shown, one side being worked a little way and then the other. The shorter stakes go in as required and

75

TECHNIQUE

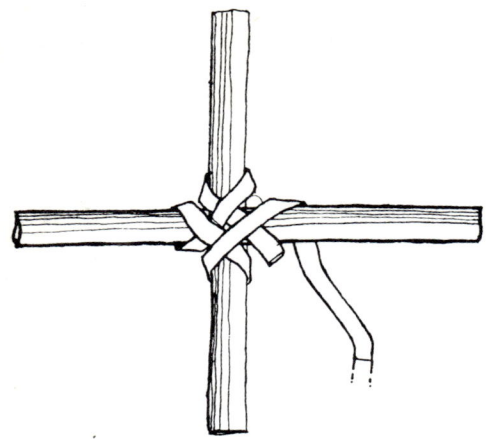

the randing weave changes to accommodate them. Some packing (48) will be needed to keep the weaving the same width. The last few inches at the centre should be quite straight so that the basket is neat to look into. It will be seen in the illustration that a round turn has to be taken

FIG. 130

round the rim every now and then and that the flat weaver must twist as it comes from underneath the rim so that the right side is always uppermost. (This drawing is not to scale. The two foundation rings are always much thicker than the stakes.)

Handles may be lapped or left plain. In the shoe basket (134) the handle ring is made of a twist of willow not of

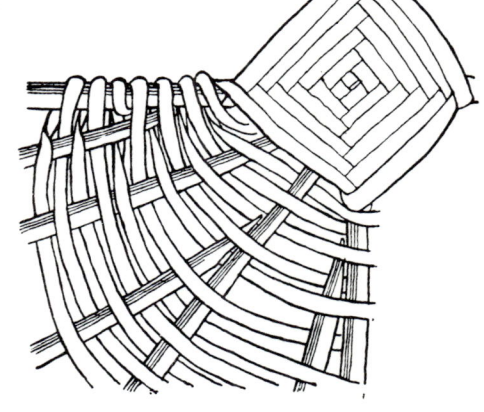

FIG. 131

the single rod. The ends lie flat at the bottom of the basket. This is elegant but rather more difficult to do.

Another method of setting cane to a given shape is to draw the outline on a plank or board and knock in small nails at intervals along it. Damp cane may then be bent round the outside of the nails and left to dry there. Damp cane wound round a broom handle will set in a spiral and keep its shape when dry.

Thicker cane, whether glossy or matt is best bent into shape over a gas flame. It must be kept on the move or it will burn. The frames of cane furniture are made in this way but the amateur needs skill, care and practice.

132   Skye Hen or Ose Basket (*see page 132*)

133   Work Basket (*see page 132*)

134 Shoe Basket, Hebrides *(see page 132)*

3. DESIGN

THE DESIGN of modern basketware in this country is, in general, poor. When it is not it has often originated in Scandinavia. There is a real need for trained designers to come into the field of basket design, both in furniture and domestic ware.

Many people going abroad will have been struck by the imaginative use of other materials with basketwork for fashion baskets. The Italians in particular are alive to the possibilities of using traditional spale and willow shapes in new ways. These have a real chic where much of their strawwork has a meretricious charm and much more is downright horrid, which does not prevent it being bought by tourists in huge quantities.

There is no need for us to borrow ideas from other countries; we have well-trained young designers with fertile brains and our traditional baskets are magnificent. But one must have some knowledge of the technique before one can design basketwork and this is seldom taught in art schools. It is obvious that to be economically worthwhile, handmade objects involving any craft techniques, when designed by trained designers, must come into the prestige class. The time may come when we shall insist on paying high prices for handmade domestic basketware and there would seem to be little point in wasting a craftsman's skill making the ugly and cheap as we do today. The value of well-designed handmade things is recognised in this country by a few people but not yet, as in Sweden and Denmark, by the many. Yet an industrial country such as ours which allows its crafts to die out will lose something vital and precious which once gone will never return. From time to time there must be renewals of interest and enthusiasm if the crafts and craftsmen are not to become crusted and anachronistic.

At present, if you ask the British journeyman working on his plank what basket in his repertoire he most admires he will probably tell you the florist's basket (145) which was high fashion in 1900. So when the trade sets out to design a piece of modern basketware its standard is not the great traditional baskets of everyday but a Victorian fernholder or basket chair. To that is grafted on the style known as "contemporary" which in basketry means plywood, coloured plastic and bleached centre cane (144 and 146).

An offshoot of this is that recipes for such things are sold in pamphlet form in shops selling craft materials. They tempt amateurs to buy materials

DESIGN

without teaching them anything worth knowing or providing them with anything worth possessing. The "Do-It Yourself" movement is a lucrative business to men without an artistic conscience and the public unfortunately seldom stops to ask if what it is doing itself is worth doing.

Yet there is no reason why the amateur should not make good baskets. Basketry is being taught in many schools and recreational institutes. But is it being well taught? Sometimes, yes, from a technical point of view, sometimes no. Basketry design is rarely taught at all; the same old baskets are turned out and the "homecraft" magazines and pamphlets are copied.

What should one look for in a good design?

Usefulness, strength, shape, texture and colour, right use of the material and craftsmanship.

Usefulness. Turn to the photographs of professionally made baskets (2, 4–13, 112–116, 124–127, 132–136) and see how many jobs baskets do, and then turn to Figs. 152–165. To employ oneself there is no need to make rubbish.

Strength. A beginner need not make a weak flabby cane wastepaper basket with a scalloped border; it is just as easy to make a strong one with a 3-rod plain border that will not come undone with constant lifting to empty. Strength is not only a matter of the thickness of the material, it comes from a knowledge of technique.

The amateur has generally to use centre cane for his baskets because of the difficulties in preparing willow and also because willow requires greater strength of hand and arm as well as greater skill. For lightness, strength and resilience willow is incomparable. It is also beautiful and full of life. On the other hand centre cane has elasticity and is easier to manipulate. With it an amateur can do things which only the finest willow-worker can do with willow.

Where willow has the advantage over cane in fine basketware is in strength for weight. This is something the public is inclined to forget. Centre cane shopping baskets and picnic baskets are often asked to carry far too much and break down. No cane shopper should be expected to carry 6 lb. of vegetables and 3 pints of milk every day. If it is, its life will be short. We have a long willow tradition in this country, so we tend to work cane like willow, also perhaps to use cane baskets with the carelessness accorded to willow ones. For the same reason we blame foreign maize and palm baskets when they give way, forgetting that in their countries of origin they are treated like paper carrier bags.

A roped or drop handle is stronger than a lapped one because it is worked into or over the side of the basket. A lapped handle depends on pegs and ties. But a handle which is part of the construction, as in a round frame

135 Tray (see page 132)

136 Tea Basket (*see page 132*)

137 Creelagh, Highlands and Islands of Scotland (*see page 132*)

138 Birdcage (*see page 133*)

139 Cradle (*see page 133*)

DESIGN

basket (see Figs. 5, 10 and 13), is strongest of all. A domed base adds strength, so do leagues and, in a cane basket, willow sticks and stakes.

Shape. Taste is a difficult thing to argue about because the good taste of one half-century is the bad taste of the next, but a sense of a good shape is different. It is not inborn, but can only be cultivated, by looking, if possible by drawing and when one is learning to be a craftsman, by touch. The best way to learn about the good shapes of baskets is to look at them and also at pottery. There are many good pots to be seen in museums and exhibitions and a visit to a local pottery will teach one a lot. The relationship between baskets and pots may be seen by looking at Figs. 127, 133, 153, 154, 163. All these are pot shapes. Having learnt to recognise a good simple shape one has to learn to make it.

The shape of a basket is determined by its upsett, that is: the first inch of weaving that setts the stakes up after they leave the base (140).

An upsett such as A could never become a bowl-shape however hard one pulls out the stakes above it. B will make a wide bowl, C will make a plate or a very wide bowl, but D will make a narrow bowl, a barrel shape or a wide-mouthed basket. E, an upsett that slants inwards, will never make anything and must be undone.

In France, Italy and the Far East much canework is done over wooden moulds. The most complicated bulges and curves can be made by this method. Amateur basketmakers often wish to make these forms and wonder why English craft books are of no use to them. This is not our way. Our tradition is different. It may surprise some people to know that English

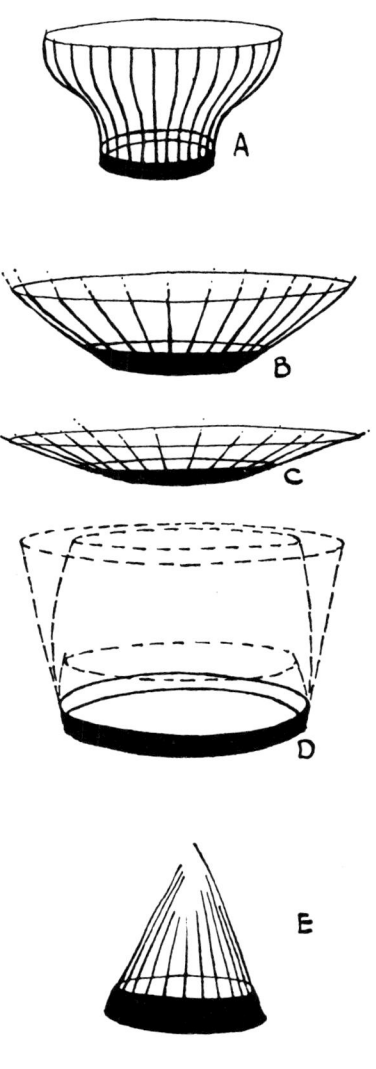

FIG. 140

85

DESIGN

baskets are greatly admired in Italy and some of the finest are exported there.

Texture. By texture, we mean the appearance of the surface of a basket. Good texture can only be achieved by practice because first and foremost it depends on smooth even weaving and finish. Variations in texture are achieved by the use of varying thicknesses of material and in the use of different strokes. It is a general rule that a basket shall have a wale to upsett and another to finish the side before bordering. Besides its decorative value a wale is a great strengthener and orders the stakes better than a rand or slew.

Flat cane or willow skeins give interesting effects, though large areas will not be so strong as round cane or rods. It is sometimes possible to buy skeins from a craftsman and to work them over cane stakes. True skeinwork is very beautiful and intricate, and is being done again in Western Germany. There are still one or two craftsmen who can make the woven skeined chair-seats in damask patterns. Some of this work is being done on modern Italian chairs and it would be pleasing to see it revived in this country. Plaited rush used to be used with willow on linen baskets and can be used with cane, so can plaited raffia. Straw plait has a lively sheen but has little strength or wearing quality. Buff willow goes admirably with cane and presents no difficulty in class work if it is used for bottom sticks and liners only, since it can be cut up before soaking. (See RECIPES III, IV, VII.)

Colour. The use of colour in willow basketry in this country is limited to its natural range of brown, white and buff. The dying of white willow has hardly been done yet, though the specially produced I.C.I. dyes (see APPENDIX A) give brilliant colour for a small cost.

Centre cane well worked is an attractive material. Like some people it gains character with age, but it has not the lively natural quality of willow. Varnish gives it a nasty texture and paint makes it more artificial than it is already. The introduction of plastic and enamelled cane has not helped towards good design, it is not a living material and has not the same tensile qualities, thus it is usually employed in bits and bobs and the effects are irritating. (See Fig. 146.) After a year or two it appears to perish, and breaks or unwinds.

The use of buff or brown willows with cane will give warmth and life. Palembang also is a pleasant reddish brown and glossy lapping cane gives a pale gold. Many people try to dye centre cane with fabric dyes but these are not fast and are seldom strong enough. There are six good colours in the I.C.I. range (APPENDIX A) and these can be mixed to produce many others, even brown and black. They are very cheap and easy to use. With such dyes available it is possible to use colour in broad bands, outlining them with

141 Willow Rattle
(*see page 133*)

142 Doll's Chair and Sofa (*see page 133*)

143 Doll's Cradle (*see page 133*)

EXAMPLES OF DOUBTFUL DESIGN

144 Plant Pot Holders, 1959. Is this Basketmaking?
(see page 133)

145 The Gainsborough— the Fashion in 1900
(see page 133)

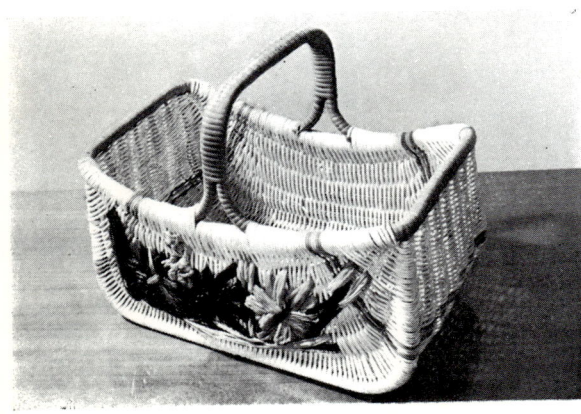

146 Heavy and Bulky Shopper in Cane, Plastic and Raffia
(see page 133)

DESIGN

yellow or dark brown, going for the bright contrasts that are the fashion in modern furnishing. (See RECIPE I.) A new field of design is open here and we can now rival the eye-catching colours of foreign baskets and perhaps revive the trade in coloured and gilded baskets which went on in the first and second centuries between Britain and Rome!

The Right Use of Material. Bernard Leach, the potter, once said that the craftsman should honour his material. This is not only a poetic statement but a practical one. Material can be used for right and wrong purposes and only a knowledge of it can tell one what they are. You cannot make a silk purse out of a sow's ear but good sows win prizes. New synthetic materials are being produced all the time and it is not easy to decide whether and on what grounds they should be used with natural materials. Often the questions are not asked; cheapness, speed in working and mere eye-catching decide the worker. It is possible to use some canework techniques with wire and plastic threads and in general this is more successful than attempts to mix them with cane and willow.

Craftsmanship. Craftsmanship is knowing how to do something, refusing to do it less well than one can, knowing one's material and giving to everything made what may be called finish.

Where the amateur has an advantage over the professional is in the time he has to spend. He can do more elaborate work because his time is not money. (See RECIPE VIII.) But in common with the professional he must have practice. There is an intoxication in having made something, but like most intoxications it is a dangerous feeling blinding the maker to self-criticism. A basket may do good service but it may still be a bad basket. Cane is a misleading material and it appears easy to handle, as indeed it is compared with willow, but perfectly even weaving, straight stakes and perfect finish require long practice. The old workshop saying that "there is no such thing as a pair of baskets" is a fair comment on the matter of shape. Every amateur should know the dimensions of his basket before he begins to make it and work with the ruler at his elbow. A basket which turns out much larger by the time the border is reached may have to have a poor mean border because the length of stakes allowed has been used up in the spread of the sides.

The master craftsman can make anything from a laundry hamper to an eel trap, though he will usually have his speciality. The amateur, especially the female one, has limitations and they may be simply of physical strength. Not all of us have strong hands and forearms. It is useless to try to make big baskets with thin material, it is better to buy them.

Finish gives an inevitability to any piece of craftwork, whether a pot, a basket, a leather bag, a knitted sock, a piece of embroidery or papering a room. What is it? The difference between the handmade and the homemade.

DESIGN

Clean endings and beginnings, the beauty of order which is only achieved by competence, by craftsmanship. Those who cannot see it have not achieved it yet.

The Design of an actual Basket

First read pages 80 to 90.
How does one design a basket?
First draw or plan the dimensions of base, top and sides (147). These may be simply a list of figures with the picture in the mind. As an example:

	Round		Oval
Base	5 ins. diameter	Base	9 ins. × 5 ins.
Height	8 ins.	Height	$7\frac{1}{2}$ ins.
Top	7 ins. diameter	Top	$13\frac{1}{2}$ ins. × $8\frac{1}{2}$ ins.

Materials. The choice of the sizes of materials may be helped by a simple workshop rule:

  Bottom sticks 4 or more sizes thicker than the stakes.
  Stakes and liners twice as thick as the wales.
  Wales twice as thick as the weavers.

Translated into centre cane:

  Bottom sticks of No. 12.   No. 10.
  Stakes and liners of No. 8.   No. 6.
  Wales of No. 6.   No. 4.
  Weavers of No. 4.   No. 2.

A perfectly satisfactory basket can be made with wales and weavers of the same size.

The weavers must never master the stakes and no beginner should attempt to make a basket with stakes and weavers the same thickness.

In slewing with cane (Fig. 35) it is better to use a thinner cane than for randing, unless the stakes and liners are exceptionally strong.

The overall choice will be determined by the size of the projected basket, its ultimate use and the sort of wear it is likely to get.

DESIGN

Length of Bottom Sticks and Stakes for a Round Basket.
Bottom Sticks. There is no rule about numbers.
A small *willow* shopper might have a 5-in. base for which cut 5 sticks 7 ins. long from the butts of 2–3-ft. willows.
A small *cane* shopper might have 8 sticks 7 ins. long cut from No. 12 cane.
Stakes. The *number* of stakes for a round basket is usually four times the number of sticks plus or minus one, to give an uneven number.
Their *length* is determined by:

Insertion into the base	2 ins.
Height of finished basket, for example	8 ins.
Extra for any curve or flow	1 in.
Border (see TECHNIQUE), for example	9 ins.
Total length	20 ins.

In a cane basket the stakes are cut exactly to size, with an inch or two extra. In a willow one the rods must be of the right size to have the required length without using the tips.

Weaving Materials. The amount required is a question of practical experience rather than rule. In preparing materials for a willow basket it is better to have too much than too little because of the time required for mellowing.

For cane baskets a study of the RECIPE section will give a fair idea.

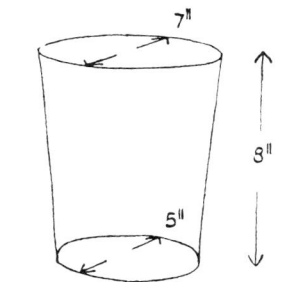

AN OVAL BASKET

The design of an oval basket is more complicated than a round one. Everything depends on the base and the design of the slath. For this there are no set rules. The simplest and most usual type is the one at Fig. 56.

The number of bottom sticks also determines the number of stakes and since there is always more "flow" at the ends than the sides, there must be more

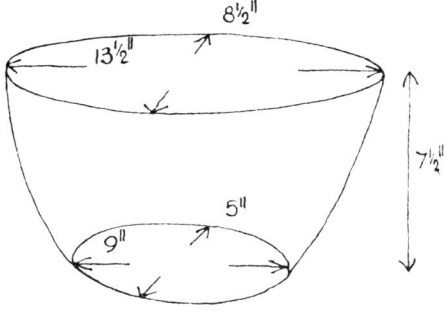

FIG. 147

DESIGN

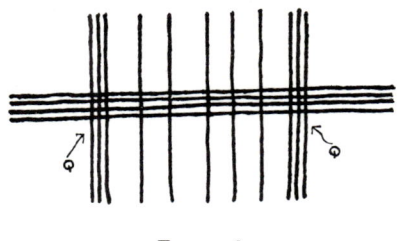

FIG. 148

stakes at the ends. Otherwise by the time the top is reached the end stakes will be further apart than the side ones and the border will be uneven. It will be seen that the oval slath consists of a number of short stakes having a lesser number of long ones put through them. An oval basket with wide ends should have perhaps 4 long sticks and a group of 3 short ones at either end with single ones between (Fig. 148). A more upright basket should have 3 long stakes and 2 or 3 short ones in the end groups (149).

A base measuring 9 ins. × 6 ins. will have long sticks $10\frac{1}{2}$ ins. and short ones $7\frac{1}{2}$ ins., allowing $1\frac{1}{2}$ ins. to spare. To make the base illustrated in Fig. 56 (without the league X), 3 long sticks and 7 short ones are needed. The *vital measurement* in making any oval base is that of the length of the slath, Q to Q in Figs. 148 and 149, when the only known measurement is the final size of the base (9 ins. × 6 ins.).

It is obtained thus:

(a) Place the long sticks together side by side and measure them. In No. 12 cane they measure $\frac{1}{2}$ in.
(b) The width of the finished base is 6 ins., and it is made up of $5\frac{1}{2}$ ins. of weaving + $\frac{1}{2}$ in. as at (a).
(c) Since there will be the same amount of weaving all the way round the base, that is at the ends as well as the sides, the length of Q-Q must be 9 ins., less $5\frac{1}{2}$ ins., that is $3\frac{1}{2}$ ins.
(d) The make-up of the base is shown at Fig. 150.

Do not be confused by the figure $2\frac{3}{4}$ ins. $2\frac{3}{4}$ ins. is half of $5\frac{1}{2}$ ins. There is $2\frac{3}{4}$ ins. of weaving on each side and at each end.

Staking-up and the Number of Stakes and Liners (151). Again there are no hard and fast rules about staking-up an oval basket, but a simple one to remember is that the bottom sticks at the sides of the base each have one stake (the Xs) and those at the ends have two, one on either side (the Os). Fig. 151 has a total of 30 stakes.

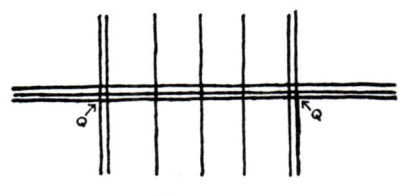

FIG. 149

DESIGN

A boat-shaped oval will have longer stakes at the ends. A cradle, with a hood, will have longer stakes at one end. As for a round basket, the *length* of the stakes is calculated by:

Inserted part into the base.
Height of the finished basket.
Any extra for curve or flow.
Border.

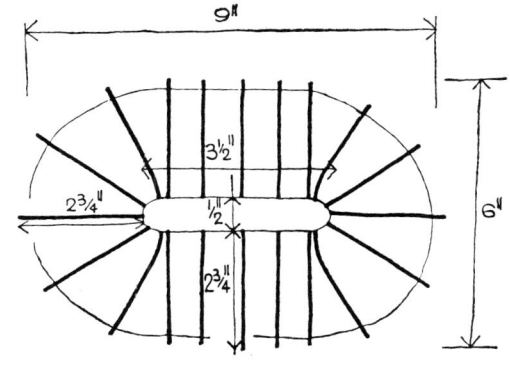

Fig. 150

A cane basket may have liners to the stakes. If these are to be cut off before bordering they should be calculated by:

The height of the finished basket.
Extra for curve or flow.
1 in. or so of spare.

If they are to be used in the border, make them the same length as the stakes, less the part inserted into the base.

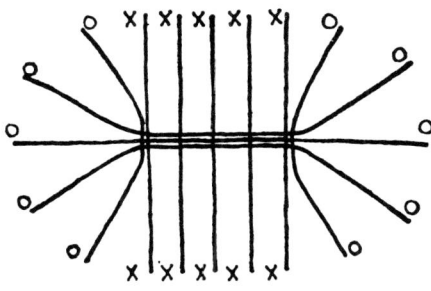

Fig. 151

These stake and liner measurements would be the same for *a wooden base* with holes but an extra 3 ins. or more would be added for working the foot border. (See TECHNIQUE.)

Weaves, Handles, Colour and Trimmings. All these are at the designer's will and have been discussed under their own headings. Fancy weaves are

93

DESIGN

always shown off at their best by large areas of plain randing. A fancy band is usually off-set by two or three rounds of waling above and below it. It should be remembered that an unprotected stake is always a weakness. A cane basket when it breaks will go at the place where the stakes are woven with weaker material. The ends of a trac border break off or a scalloped one come out. Fitching is weaker than solid weaving.

Proportion. Here one can only repeat the remarks made about *Shape* on page 85. The height of a narrow straight shape such as a linen basket will deceive the eye. The top should be an inch or two bigger than the bottom, or it will appear to run in.

152 Wastepaper Basket (*Instructions: page 99*)

153 Simple Round Workbasket (*Instructions: page 100*)

154 Round Workbasket in Cane and Buff Willow (*Instructions: page 101*)

155 Tall Oval Shopping Basket (*Instructions: page 102*)

4. RECIPES

I.   WASTEPAPER BASKET   Figure 152
            (Centre Cane on a Wooden Base)
                Using dyed cane.

Materials:

    7-in. round wooden base with holes.
    3 ozs. No. 5 centre cane for stakes cut 17 ins. long and liners 14 ins. long.
    $\frac{1}{4}$ lb. No. 4 natural.
    1 oz. No. 4 in colour A.
    1 oz. No. 4 in colour B.
    $\frac{1}{2}$ oz. No. 4 in colour C.
    The model has Chinese pink for colour A.
            Deep blue for colour B.
            Bright yellow for colour C.

Sides:

    Cut stakes and liners to the number of holes.
    Foot border (Fig. 92).
    Upsett with 4 canes in colour B, 4 rounds. (See Fig. 43.)
    Insert liners.
    One round with colour C (Fig. 43).
    Three rounds with colour A (Fig. 43).
    Rand with natural cane until 6 ins. high from the base (Fig. 33).
    1 round waling (Fig. 43) in colour C.
    4 rounds waling in colour B.
    1 round waling in colour C.
    3 rounds waling in colour A.
    With natural cane work 1 round of pairing (Fig. 46) taking stakes and bye-stakes separately.

Border:

    Border with 3-rod plain (see Figs. 71–74) and a back trac (Fig. 76).

Measurements:

    Height 8 ins.
    Across top, inside: 9 ins.; outside: $10\frac{1}{2}$ ins.

RECIPES

II.   SIMPLE ROUND WORKBASKET   Figure 153
                (Centre Cane)

This basket was made by a student. It has its faults, but the shape is so good that one can forgive them all.

Materials:
    ½ oz. No. 12 for bottom and lid sticks.
    3 ozs. No. 5 for stakes and liners.
    6 ozs. No. 3 for weaving.

Base:
    7 ins. diameter, paired (see Fig. 46).
    8 sticks 8½ ins. long (see Figs. 49 and 52).

Side:
    33 stakes No. 5, 14 ins. long.
    33 liners No. 5, 12 ins. long.
    Upsett with 1 round of 5-rod wale and 4 rounds of 3-rod (Figs. 38–42, page 58).
    Put in liners and rand (Fig. 33) until 4½ ins. high and 9 ins. across.
    Work 1 round of 3-rod wale, add two more weaving canes and work a ledge (Fig. 109).
    Border with a trac, using the pairs (Fig. 69). (The ledge given in Fig. 110 may be used. This is worked after the border.)

Lid:
    8 sticks of No. 12 measuring 1½ ins. more than the diameter of the top of the basket, 16 extra sticks half the length (Fig. 108).
    If diameter is less than 9 ins., extra sticks are not needed.
    Pair for 5 rounds.
    Cut off 1 cane and rib-rand (Fig. 37) with right side of lid towards you. The diameter before bordering must be 1 in. less than the diameter of the basket inside, above the ledge.

Border: (Underside towards you.)
    Insert a pair of No. 5 stakes 5 ins. long on either side of each stick and extra stick, and work a trac in front of 1, behind 1, in front of 1.

Handles: (Fig. 102.)

Final Measurements:
- 6 ins. high.
- 11 ins. across top.
- 7½ ins. across base.

A smaller basket can be made on a 6-in. base; 5½ ins. high; 9 ins. across top.

III. ROUND WORKBASKET   Figure 154
(Centre Cane and Buff Willow)
For texture, colour and shape.

Materials:
- 2 ozs. No. 5 for stakes.
- 3 ozs. No. 3 for weaving.
- ¼ lb. 2 ft.–2½ ft. fine buff willows for sticks and liners.

Base:
7 buff willow sticks 7 ins. long (thickness of No. 8 cane). (See page 26 for treatment of willow.)
Paired Diameter 5 ins. (Figs. 52 and 46).

Sides:
29 stakes No. 5 10¼ ins. long.
29 buff willow liners, same thickness, 6½ ins. long.
Upsett with 1 round of 5-rod wale and 3 rounds of 3-rod (Figs. 38–42, and page 38).
Insert liners and slew (Fig. 35) with 2 canes to a height of 4¾ ins. following the shape in the illustration. The stakes and liners must be wetted and mellowed for a short time before the inward curve is made.
Work 1 round of 5-rod wale.
Then 3 more rounds of slewing, still curving inwards.
Cut off willows and work a trac border, behind 1, in front of 1, behind 1. (See Fig. 68 and Notes.)

Lid: (a trunk cover)
8 willow sticks 1½ ins. longer than the diameter of the top and 1 stick half the length, slyped at one end. (See Fig. 54.)
Pair 3 rounds to divide the sticks after tying the slath and slew the lid until it is the same size as the top of the basket.

RECIPES

Insert a 7-in. stake of No. 5 on either side of each lid stick and work 1 round of 3-rod wale taking in each block of 2 canes and 1 willow.
Cut off willows, turn stakes at right angles.
With the right side towards you work 5 rounds of 3-rod wale, testing the lid to see that it fits over the basket. (See page 64 on *Lids*.)
Border with a 3-rod plain border (Figs. 71–74), leaving the ends on the outside.

Handle:

A loop of natural calf leather 1 in. wide and 8 ins. long, with the ends tapered and taken through and tied inside the lid.

Final Measurements:

Height to top of 5-rod ledge: 5 ins.
Height to top of basket: $5\frac{1}{2}$ ins.
Total height of basket to top of lid: $7\frac{1}{2}$ ins.
Across base: $5\frac{1}{4}$ ins.
Across basket at widest part of curve when $3\frac{1}{4}$ ins. high: $7\frac{3}{4}$ ins.
Across top of basket inside: 7 ins.
Across lid inside: $7\frac{1}{2}$ ins.

IV. TALL OVAL SHOPPING BASKET Figure 155
(Centre Cane and Buff Willow)

This basket could be made in all cane, but the buff willow gives colour and strength.

Materials: From 3-ft. buff willows:

4 bottom sticks, $11\frac{1}{2}$ ins., cut from the butts.
11 bottom sticks, $6\frac{1}{4}$ ins., cut from the butts.
42 liners, 11 ins., cut from the rods giving a thickness of No. 4 to No. 7 cane.
3 ozs. No. 5 cane cut into 38 stakes 20 ins. long and two leagues 45 ins. long.
7–8 ozs. No. 3 for weaving.
1 length No. 8 cane for core of upsett.
2 pieces No. 16 cane $28\frac{1}{2}$ ins. long.
2 lengths No. 6 chair cane.
2 lengths No. 4 chair cane.

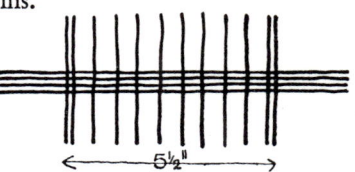

Fig. 156

RECIPES

Base: (See page 43 and pages 26 and 27 for treatment of willow.)

Make the slath 5½ ins. long (see Figs. 156 and 56) and weave the base, putting in two leagues.

Base measures 10 ins. × 5 ins.

Sides:

Double-stake 6 sticks at each end and single-stake the rest. (See Figs. 61 and 151.)

Upsett as Fig. 62 and then with 3 rounds of 3-rod wale (Figs. 38–42). Put in the liners with the belly of the willows to the inside of the basket.

Slew with two canes (Figs. 34 and 35) using a second pair because of the even number of stakes. When 9 ins. high the basket measures 12 ins. × 8 ins. on the inside.

Work 3 rounds of 3-rod wale.

Border: (See Figs. 71–74, 75 and 68.)

The trac of in front of 1, behind 1 is worked on the inside after the follow-on trac.

Handles: (See Figs. 100, 101 and 99.)

Final Measurements:

Height: 10½ ins.
Top inside: 12 ins. × 8 ins.

V.   LARGE SHOPPING BASKET   Figure 158
(Cane reinforced with White Willow)

This basket could be made in all cane, but is stronger with willow. The design is traditional.

Materials: From 3-ft. white willows:

4 bottom sticks, 13½ ins., cut from the butts.

11 bottom sticks, 9 ins., cut from the butts.

46 liners, 7 ins. long, cut from the rods giving a thickness of No. 6 to 8 cane.

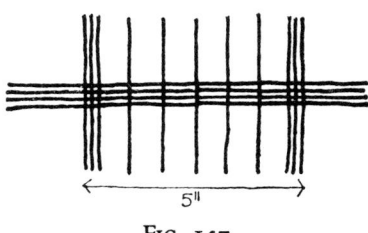

Fig. 157

RECIPES

    3 ozs. No. 8 cane, cut into 46 17-in. stakes.
    2 ozs. No. 5 for the wales.
    6 ozs. No. 3 for randing.
    3 pieces 8-mm. handle cane, approx. 33 ins. long.
    2 or 3 lengths glossy lapping cane.
    1 length No. 6 chair cane for listing.

Base: (See page 43.)
    Make the slath 5 ins. long (see Figs. 157 and 56) tying and randing (Fig. 34) with No. 3 cane until base measures 12 ins. × 7½ ins.

Sides:
    Double-stake the end sticks and single-stake the seven middle sticks on either side.
    (See Figs. 61 and 151.)
    Upsett with No. 5 cane as in Fig. 62 (or with a simple 5-rod wale) and a single chain wale (Figs. 44 and 45) using 4 weavers in front of 3 and behind 1.
    Insert liners.
    Rand (Fig. 34) with No. 3 until basket is 5 ins. high. After 1 in. insert 6 bow marks (see page 64) at central stakes and at the third stake away from these, on either side.
    Finish with 2 rounds of chain waling as before.
    Cut off liners and work a 4-rod plain border (Fig. 77).

Handle:
    Remove bow marks and insert handle canes, nailing together at centre and sides.
    Follow Figs. 97, 98.
    Peg all three bows. (See page 59.)

Measurements:
    Height of basket: 6 ins.
    Height to top of handle: 12½ ins.
    Length of basket outside border: 16 ins.
    Breadth of basket outside border: 12 ins.

158 Large Shopping Basket (*Instructions: page 103*)

159 All-purpose Plate (*Instructions: page 113*)

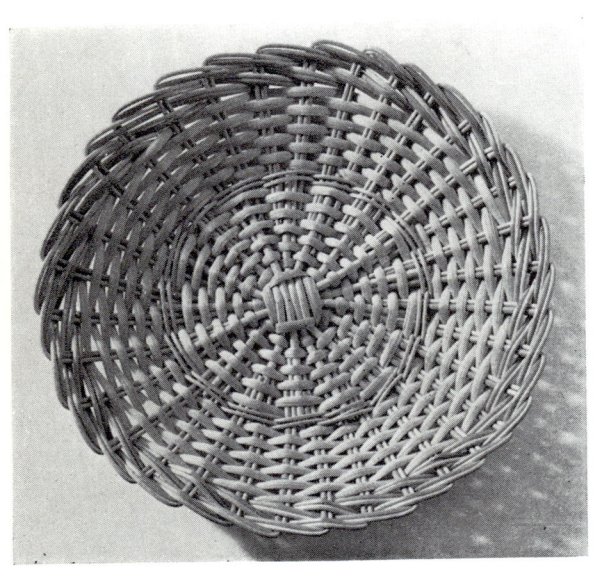

160 Swedish Plate in Cane and Buff Willow

(*Instructions: page 113*)

161 Lidded Picnic Basket (*Instructions: page 114*)

162 Wine Cradle (*Instructions: page 116*)

163 Round Linen Basket *(Instructions: page 118)*

164 Strong Shopping Basket with Rope Handle
(Instructions: page 120)

165 Miniatures: Cradle, Shopping Basket and Carpet Beater
(*Instructions: pages 122 and 123*)

166 Bread or Fruit Bowl and a Cane Rattle (*Instructions: pages 124 and 125*)

167 Ball, Interlaced Dish and Mat (*Instructions: pages 125 and 126*)

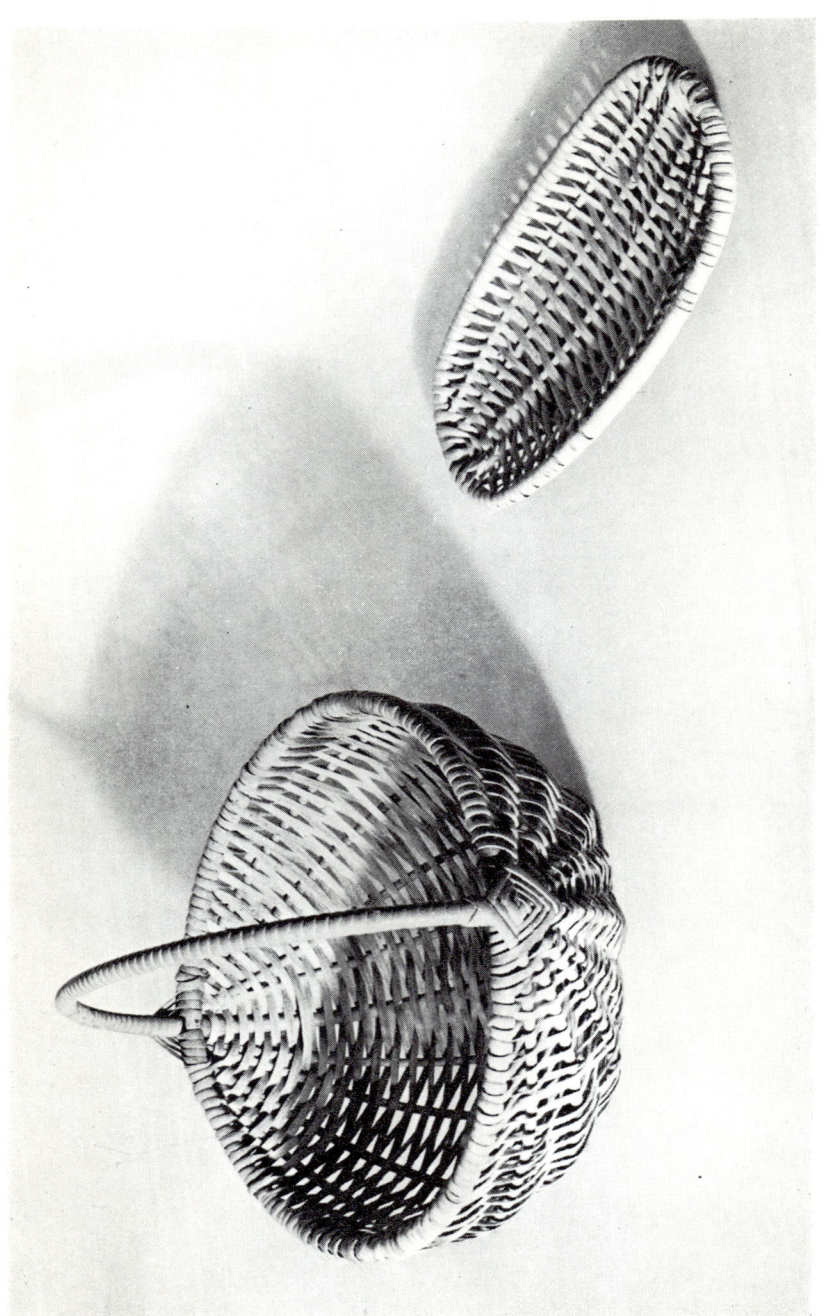

168 Light Frame Shopping Basket and Frame Dish (*Instructions: pages 127 and 128*)

RECIPES

VI.   ALL-PURPOSE PLATE   Figure 159
(A small Centre Cane version of a buff willow tray)

Material:
   10 pieces No. 12 cane, 9½ ins. long, for bottom sticks.
   ½ oz. No. 2 cane
   1½ ozs. No. 4 cane.
   2 ozs. No. 5—Cut 40 stakes 9½ ins. long.
   1 short length No. 4 chair cane for decoration of slath.

Base: (See Figs. 49, 53 and 52.)
   Begin weaving with No. 2 cane. After dividing all canes singly, pair for 1 more round.
   Rib-rand (Fig. 37) for 8 rounds with No. 2.
   Change to No. 4 for 12 rounds.
   And to No. 5 until base measures 8½ ins. across.

Sides:
   Insert 2 stakes to each bottom stick.
   Upsett with No. 4 (page 46) 1 round of 4-rod wale in front of 3 and behind 1 and 4 rounds 3-rod wale (Figs. 38-42 and page 38).

Border: (See Figs. 71-75.)

Measurements:
   8½ ins. across inside.
   1 in. high.

VII.   SWEDISH PLATE   Figure 160
(Cane and Buff Willow)

This basket is a direct copy of a Swedish one but is an object lesson in good design.

Materials:
   No. 12 cane cut into 8 bottom sticks 7 ins. long and 1 of 4 ins. long.
   1 oz. No. 5 cane cut into 33 stakes 9 ins. long.
   1 oz. No. 3 cane.
   1 oz. Matt lapping cane.
   18 ins.–2 ft. buff willows. Cut 33 stakes 9 ins. long, roughly the thickness of No. 5, from the rods.

RECIPES

Base: (See Fig. 54.)
Tie and Rand (Fig. 33) for 10 rounds with lapping cane.

Side:
Before cutting off bottom sticks insert stakes in pairs of 1 cane, 1 willow—the willow always to the right, with the right side of the base facing—2 pairs per stick except for 1 single pair to give the odd number. Push stakes in for $1\frac{1}{2}$ ins.
With No. 3 cane pair (Fig. 46) twice round over the blocks of 2 pairs and 1 bottom stick. Cut off the bottom sticks, closely.
Rand the pairs with lapping cane for 9 rounds, first securing the end with a spring clothes peg and kinking the willows to get the sett-up from the base.

Border:
A trac with the pairs of in front of 1, behind 1, in front of 1, behind 1 (Fig. 69). The willows should be pricked to bend at $\frac{7}{8}$ in. above the weaving, and slightly twisted at the finish of the border to prevent cracking.

Measurement:
$9\frac{3}{4}$ ins. across.

N.B. Willows must be kept mellow all the time, particularly when the border is worked. (See page 26.)

VIII.   LIDDED PICNIC BASKET   Figure 161
(Centre Cane)

This basket and its lid are made on a scallomed base. It is not for beginners.

Materials:
$6\frac{1}{2}$-mm. handle cane.
1 oz. No. 12 cane.
5 ozs. No. 6 for stakes and liners.
1 lb. No. 3 for all weaving.
1 piece of lapping cane.
Leather for harness.

RECIPES

Base:

Make a shaping board (see Fig. 60) 15 ins. × 3½ ins. with rounded ends. On this make a hoop with 6½-mm. cane (see pages 45 and 46) allowing an overlap of 4 ins. 5 scalloms of No. 12 cane run from end to end. Rand with No. 2 (see Fig. 33).

Sides:

49 stakes No. 6, 15 ins. long.
49 liners No. 6, 10 ins. long.
Stakes are slyped and driven into the frame using a bodkin. (Figs. 63 and 64 show this when a rectangular base is made.)
Upsett with 6 rounds 3-rod wale (see Figs. 38–42).
16 rounds randing.
2 rounds 3-rod wale.
3½ ins. slewing, 2 canes (see Figs. 35 and 34).
2 rounds 3-rod wale.
23 rounds randing.
4 rounds 3-rod wale.
Cut off liners.
* 1 round 4-rod wale. (See *Measurements*.)
4 rounds pairing (see Fig. 46) setting the work inwards.
Border with a trac of behind 1, in front of 1, behind 1 (see Fig. 68).

Thermos partitions (optional):

Two pieces of 6½ mm. are nailed 4½ ins. in from the ends of the basket, just below the 4-rod wale, from side to side, and are lapped with flat cane; the end is first passed to the outside of the basket, over the nail and inside again.

Measurements (outside):

10 ins. high.
Bottom: 16 ins. × 5 ins.
* At 4-rod wale: 16 ins. × 6½ ins.
Top: 14½ ins. × 5½ ins.

Lid:

Tack a piece of No. 12 cane to either side of the shaping board to make it wider. Make a base like the basket.

Sides:

56 stakes No. 6, 6 ins. long.
Work 7 rounds of 3-rod wale.
Border with 3-rod plain (see Figs. 71–74).

RECIPES

Measurements (outside):
   1½ ins. deep.
   16¼ ins. × 6¾ ins.

Harness:
   The basket illustrated has a harness of scarlet kip leather, ⅞ in. wide. The handles are double, hand-stitched, and a single strap with a buckle holds the lid on. The brass studs have split pins and the four at the base of the handles are put through the basket and hold the harness firmly to it.

Alternately:
   The basket could have drop handles of cane (see Fig. 100) and fastenings of various types (Figs. 121, 122 and 123).

IX.　　　　　WINE CRADLE　　　　　Figure 162
　　　　(A variation on a familiar design)

May be made on a wooden or a frame base (see Figs. 169 and 59). If the latter is used the shaping board should be made from the same diagram as the wooden one (Fig. 169) but ¼ in. smaller all round. The same number of stakes and the same method will be used for the rest of the cradle. The scalloms should be of No. 8 cane and the base woven with No. 3.

Materials:
   A wooden base as in Fig. 169 with 31 holes, to take No. 5 cane and 2 larger corner holes.
   1½ ozs. No. 5, cut into 31 stakes 13½ ins. long.
   2 ozs. No. 3 cane (2½ ozs. for the cane-based cradle).
   2 corner posts of white willow or No. 12 cane, 4 ins. long and 2 for the front, 6 ins. long.
   6½ mm. handle cane.
   No. 6 chair cane 2 long pieces.

Sides:
   Work a foot border behind 1, in front of 1, behind 1 (see Fig. 92). Insert the corner posts.
   Upsett. Double chain wale (see Figs. 44 and 45 and text) setting the front stakes forward and bringing stake A to the centre (see Fig. 169).
   Rand (Fig. 33) for 8 rounds.

Then pack either side (see Fig. 48) beginning at the third stake forward from the corner post and working a clear round each time between the short turns. There should be 5 short turns to each side.

8 more rounds of randing.

The cradle should then *measure* 1¾ ins. at the back and 2¾ ins. at the front.

Insert a bowmark of 6½-mm. cane at the centre back stake (see page 64).

The Notch: (See Fig. 111.)

One stake only is brought down: stake A in Fig. 169.

Upper Side:

Insert a corner post by the side of the stake on either side of the notch (Fig. 111).

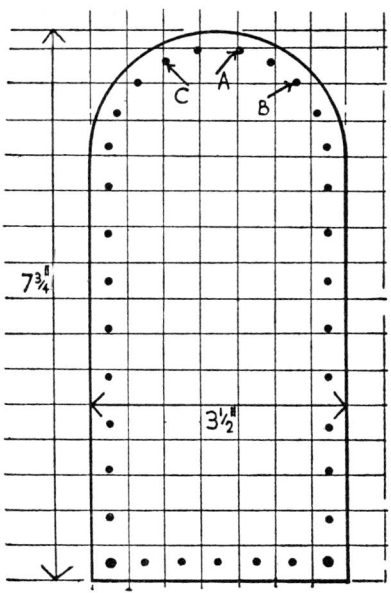

FIG. 169

Insert a bye-stake of No. 5 8½ ins. long to the front of stakes B and C. Rand for 10 rounds using the bye-stakes as stakes and making a round turn at the front corner posts at every round.

After 1 or 2 rounds put in a bowmark of 6½-mm. cane at the eighth stake forward from the back corner at either side.

Pack the sides 5 times giving 2 clear rounds between each short turn.

Double chain wale, beginning at the front right-hand post by doubling 1 pair of canes round it to make 2 pairs and laying in the third between the second and third stake. On reaching the left-hand front post, when the leading pair has gone behind it, begin the second row thus; working from right to left:

(a) Take the second pair round the post from front to back and forward again between post and stake to its left.

(b) Then take the leading pair round in front of the post and the stake to its left, behind the third stake and forward again.

(c) Cut off the third pair as it lies to the front and reinsert it between the second and third stakes in the new row.

RECIPES

Three pairs are now in sequence and the reverse movement is made automatically by working an ordinary wale from right to left.

To complete the chain wale at the right-hand post take the leading pair round it from back to front and to the inside and cut off.

Cut off the other 2 pairs on the outside.

Border:

3-rod plain (Figs. 71–74) first cutting off the back corner posts.

Handle: (Made in 2 pieces.)

The one from side to side is lapped first (see Fig. 95) without interlacing. Second has a long slype folded over the first and nailed (Fig. 101). It is lapped from front to back with single piece of No. 3 interlaced. Peg all 3 handles (see page 59).

Bind each side of the notch with chair cane before cutting off the posts and trim the front with a ring (Fig. 102) of No. 5, sewn on with chair cane.

Final Measurements:

Height at front from base: $5\frac{1}{4}$ ins.
Height at back from base: 4 ins.
Height of side-to-side handle: $9\frac{1}{2}$ ins.
Length from back to front at the border: $9\frac{1}{2}$ ins.
Width at border at widest part: 5 ins.

X.   ROUND LINEN BASKET   Figure 163
              (Centre Cane and Wooden Base)

The design is based on the oil jars of the Mediterranean.

Materials:

12-in. round wooden base with holes 1 in.–$1\frac{1}{4}$ ins. apart. (Every other hole on a ready-made base.) An uneven number of holes is preferable.
$\frac{1}{2}$ lb. No. 10 cane cut into 26-in. stakes, and liners the same length less the amount needed for the foot border.
2 lb. No. 8 for weaving.
1 oz. No. 3 for weaving lid.
1 oz. No. 5 for weaving lid.
No. 12 cane for lid sticks.
2 lengths No. 14 for handle, 9 ins. long.

RECIPES

Base:
> Work foot border (Fig. 92).

Sides:
> Upsett with 2 rounds single chain wale (4 rows) (see Figs. 44 and 45) setting out slightly. Add liners and rand (Fig. 33) until basket is 10 ins. high and 15 ins across.
> Shape in. At 12 ins. high the neck is 12 ins. across.

Neck:
> Squeeze stakes all round.
> Work one round of chain wale, holding stakes vertical in the first row; squeeze again and work second row holding stakes well out.
> Work 5 rounds of 3-rod wale (Figs. 38-42) working on the inside of the basket and keeping the neck at a wide angle.
> Using No. 5 cane, work 1 round of pairing (Fig. 46) to divide stakes and liners.
> Work a 3-rod plain border on the edge, and then a back-trac, in front of 1, behind 1, mellowing the cane well first (Figs. 71-74 and 76).

Lid:
> Cut 8 sticks of No. 12 cane, 1 in. longer than the diameter of the lid when finished.
> Begin as for a base (Figs. 49 and 52) weaving with No. 3 cane.
> Pair twice more round after dividing sticks.
> Cut 1 bye-stake to each stick and insert (Fig. 108).
> Work 2 more rounds over the pairs and then another to divide all singly.
> Lid will have 32 sticks.
> Rib-rand (Fig. 37) for 5 rounds with No. 5 cane.
> Slype the ends of the handle canes and slip them into the last two rounds of weaving so that they lie by two adjoining stakes on either side, and continue to work over them.
> Rib-rand with No. 8 cane until lid is $\frac{3}{4}$ in. less than the required diameter.
> Cut and insert an $8\frac{1}{2}$-in. stake of No. 8 cane to each stick and work a 3-rod plain border (Figs. 71-74) working on the inside.

Handle:
> Complete as described on pages 58 and 59, with Figs. 93 and 94.

RECIPES

Lining:
    Line the basket with plastic material.

Measurements:
    Height to top of handle 16 ins.
    Height of basket to rim 14½ ins.
    Width at widest part when 10 ins. high 15 ins.
    Width at rim edge 15½ ins.

XI.   STRONG SHOPPING BASKET   Figure 164
                     WITH ROPE HANDLE

(Centre cane, split Palembang & white willow.)

If willow is hard to get it may be replaced by Palembang or centre cane.

Materials:
    ¼ lb. No. 8 cane cut into 38 stakes 23 ins. long.
    3 ozs. No. 6 cane for upsett and top wale.
    ½ lb. Palembang size 5–8, split, (see page 29) and used for weaving base and sides, but used whole as a core in all wales.
    3–4 ft. white willows cut:
    9 bottom sticks 8½ ins. from the butts.
    3 bottom sticks 14 ins. from the butts.
    38 liners about the thickness of No. 8 cane 9¼ ins. long.
    2½ yds. 3-strand hemp rope about ⅝ ins. thick or two pieces 8-mm. handle cane.

Base: (See page 43 and pages 26 and 27 for the treatment of willow.)
    Make the slath as Fig. 170.
    Bind it with split Palembang making a cross at each stake but no binds between.
    Rand the base.
    Base measures 10½ ins. × 6½ ins.

Sides:
    For staking up follow the second diagram of Fig. 170.
    Xs = single stakes, Os = double stakes, Ys = treble stakes.

RECIPES

Upsett as Fig. 62 with 5 canes of No. 6 over a core of Palembang, then with 3 rounds of 4-rod chain wale each worked over a core of Palembang. (Fig. 44.) Put in liners with the belly of the willows to the outside of the basket.

Rand with split Palembang using two pieces beginning at opposite sides because of the even number of stakes.

When 8 ins. high the basket measures 14 ins. × 10 ins. on the inside.

Work 3 rounds of chain wale as for the upsett.

Border: (See Fig. 77.)

Finish with a follow-on trac. (See Fig. 75.)

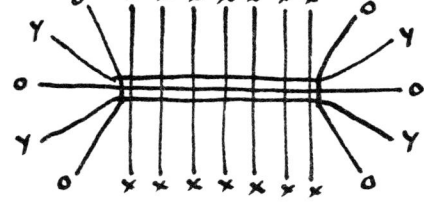

FIG. 170

Final Measurements:

Height of basket to rim: $8\frac{3}{4}$ ins.
Height to top of handle 16 ins.
Top inside rim $10\frac{1}{2}$ ins. × $14\frac{1}{2}$ ins.

Handle:

Cut $2\frac{1}{2}$ yards of rope in half. Join again to make a circle with two Shroud Knots with the ends marled and served with hemp twine. The ropes should measure 31 ins. between the two knots and must be exact. To make this consult:

Knots, Splices and Fancy Work by Charles L. Spencer or
Rope Splicing by P. W. Blandford, both published by Brown, Son and Ferguson, or The Ashley Book of Knots.

When completed sew the handle to the basket with No. 8 cane following Figure 164 and giving a tight stitch between the two halves of the knot itself.

Finally lap the centres of the two ropes together to make a hand hold,

RECIPES

using split Palembang, for 5 ins., with short pieces of Palembang interwoven under 2, over 2. (see Fig. 95) at the same time laying a piece of Palembang in the gap between the two ropes to fill it.

N.B. This basket may have a rigid cane handle lapped with Palembang.

XII. MINIATURE CRADLE Figure 165

Materials:
    A few lengths No. 1 cane.
    A few lengths No. 0 cane.
    Two short pieces of No. 8 for rockers.
    A short length of No. 2 chair cane.

Base and Sides: (These are made in one.)
    3 pieces No. 1, 15 ins. long, and 6 pieces 12 ins. long.
    (See Fig. 57.) Set outside stakes $1\frac{3}{4}$ ins. apart.
    The end stakes should be an inch longer at the hood end.
    Pair this, taking the 3 long stakes together at the ends, for 1 round.
    Open out and reverse pair (see Fig. 47) until base measures $3\frac{1}{4}$ ins. × $1\frac{1}{2}$ ins.
    Add 4 extra stakes at each end making them the same length as the rest.
    Upsett with 4 rounds of 3-rod wale.
    Add $2\frac{1}{4}$-in. liners at one end and $3\frac{1}{2}$-in. ones at the other (hood) end.
    Rand with 2 canes for 8 rounds (Fig. 34).
    Then pack the hood end for 5 turns each side (Fig. 48) beginning at the side stake next to the centre one.
    Rand for 6 rounds, curving the hood.
    Pack again 4 times beginning at one stake nearer the end than the last time.
    Work 2 rounds of 3-rod wale.

Border:
    3-pair plait (see Figs. 78–83).

Rockers:
    Damp two short pieces of No. 8 and curve.
    Sew with a cross of chair cane to the upsett at either end.

RECIPES

XIII. MINIATURE ROUND SHOPPING BASKET   Figure 165

Miniatures are good practice in handling the material.

Materials:
  A few lengths of No. 1 and No. 0 cane.
  A short piece of No. 6.

Base and Sides:
  6 pieces No. 1, 18 ins. long, for bottom sticks and stakes in one.
  (See Fig. 55.) Pair or rand until 1 in. across.
  Upsett (Figs. 38–42) with 4 rounds 3-rod wale.
  Add liners, $2\frac{3}{4}$ ins. long, No. 1.
  Rand (Fig. 33) until 2 ins. high.
  Work 2 rounds 3-rod wale.

Border: (Figs. 71–75.)

Handle:
  Bow of No. 6 and weaver of No. 0
  (see Figs. 93 and 94).

Measurements:
  Height: $2\frac{1}{4}$ ins.
  Across top, outside: $2\frac{1}{2}$ ins.
  Height to top of handle: $3\frac{3}{4}$ ins.

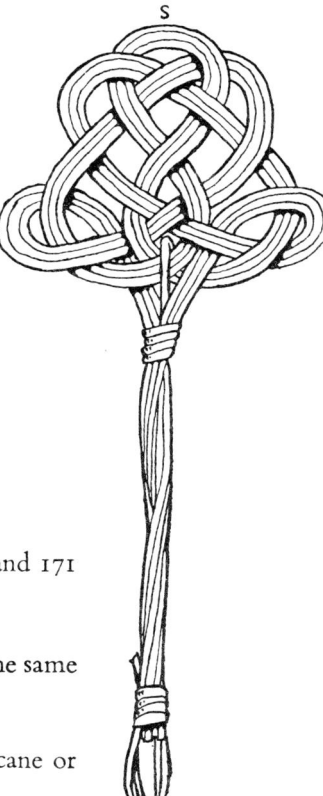

XIV. CARPET BEATER
        Figures 165 and 171
        Full Size

Materials:
  3 lengths of No. 12 cane or palembang the same thickness about 12 ft long.
  1 length of the same 3 ft. 6 ins. long.
  1 length of $6\frac{1}{2}$-mm. or 8-mm. handle cane or kubu 2 ft. 6 ins. long.
  Lapping cane.
  Wire.

FIG. 171

RECIPES

Method:
>Take the centre of one long piece of cane and follow Fig. 171, starting at S and working with both ends. When the pattern is complete, work in the other two long pieces separately, one above and one below the first.

Handle:
>Slype one end of the short No. 12, and when wet and mellow bend it over the crossing as shown. Lap it to the handle cane with wire for about 1 in. Lap all canes together with lapping cane and twist them round the handle cane. Turn up the end of the short No. 12 to make a loop and lap all together with lapping cane.

The Miniature. Fig. 165 is made of No. 1 cane. The head is $2\frac{1}{4}$ ins. long and the whole beater 7 ins. long.

XV. BREAD OR FRUIT BOWL Figure 166
(Centre Cane. Fine)

Materials:
>8 pieces No. 12 cane, 5 ins. long.
>1 oz. No. 3 cane cut into 33 stakes $10\frac{1}{2}$ ins. long.
>$1\frac{1}{2}$ ozs. No. 1 cane for weaving.

Base: (See Figs. 49–52.) $3\frac{1}{2}$ ins. across.

Sides:
>Stake up. (See Fig. 61.)
>Upsett with 1 round 5-rod wale and 3 rounds 3-rod. (Figs. 38–42 and notes with Fig. 43.)
>Rand (Fig. 33) until $1\frac{1}{4}$ ins. high and 6 ins. across.
>Work 1 round double chain wale (Figs. 44 and 45 and text).
>Rand until $2\frac{1}{4}$ ins. high and 6 ins. across.
>Complete with 1 round of 3-rod wale.

Border:
>Worked in 3 separate rounds:
>1st. A 3-rod plain border (Figs. 71–74) which brings all stakes to the outside.
>2nd. A back-trac of in front of 2, behind 1 (Fig. 76).
>3rd. Still going from right to left (as for the back-trac) take the ends under two through to the inside of the basket under the border. Pull tight.

RECIPES

Measurements:
>Across the top on the outside of the border: 6¼ ins.
>Across the top on the inside of the border: 5⅜ ins.
>Height: 2½ ins.

XVI. CANE RATTLE Figure 166

Materials:
>6 pieces No. 5 cane, 22 ins. long.
>1 piece No. 5 cane, 14 ins. long.
>No. 2 cane for weaving.
>No. 6 chair cane.

Construction:
>Put 3 through 3 as for a base (Fig. 49).
>Tie together with chair cane and add the short stake. Pair open (Fig. 54).
>Rib-rand the ball (Fig. 37) finishing with a round of pairing.
>Insert a bell or two folded pieces of tin.
>Bring stakes together and lap with chair cane, turning up the long end for a handle.
>Trim with 2 single Turk's Head rings of chair cane (see Figs. 103–107).

XVII. BALL Figure 167

Balls of this type, sometimes with more interlacing rings and more intricate patterns, are made in Java for a sort of football.

Materials:
>4 long pieces of No. 7 cane, 1 natural and the others different colours.
>Take 3 canes and make an interlaced triangle at the centres.
>With one set of ends form another triangle the same as the first and bring all canes up to the first one again. With the fourth cane weave under and over the other canes between the two triangles. This will form 4 interlocking circles. Go round and round using both ends of the canes until each circle is about 10 rounds wide.
>Spring clothes pegs will help to hold the canes in the early stages. A little glue will secure the ends inside and the ball may be varnished.

Diameter:
>4 ins, but the ball may be a larger size using thicker cane. Thinner or bleached cane is not suitable.

RECIPES

XVIII.   INTERLACED DISH   Figures 167 and 172

The interlaced figure is called an "Ocean Mat" in seaman's parlance, being usually made in rope. This dish like the mat in Fig. 167, is a central figure of 6 strands with two outer rings laced on with chair cane.

Materials:

2 or 3 long pieces of No. 5 cane.
2 or 3 pieces of No. 3 chair cane.

Construction: (See Fig. 172.)

Work flat. The centre of a length of No. 5 is at B. Lay the left hand cane D over the right hand C. Curl D round as shown and hold it down. Thread C over and under D following the dotted line. By taking the arrow end up on the right side of D you complete the figure.

Weave both ends round until it is 6 rounds wide. For lacing method see the mat on page 127.

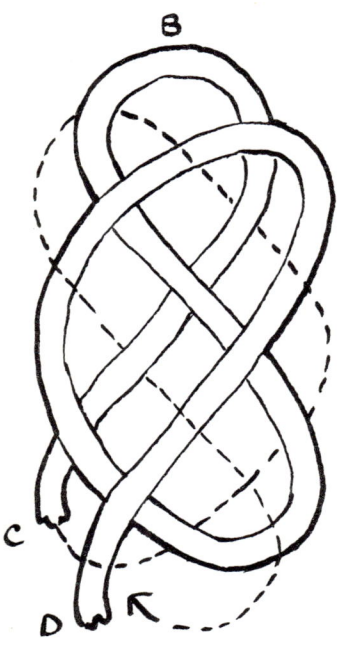

Fig. 172

Measurements:

8½ ins. × 4 ins. before adding the outer rings. (First complete figure measures ½ ins. less.)
Can be made larger and with thicker material.

XIX.   INTERLACED MAT   Figures 162 and 173

This is a copy of a mat made in Japan from a type of cane not imported here. It was dark brown in colour and the lacing was chair cane. It is in fact a flattened turk's head (see Figs. 103–106).

Materials:

2 long pieces of No. 7 cane.
1 long piece of No. 3 chair cane.

RECIPES

Construction:

It consists of a 5-sided figure (see Fig. 173) with two separate circles round the edge. The chair cane lacing is done from left to right and joins of the circles should come where they are lapped to each other, the inner circle being joined before the outer one. If Fig. 167 is studied carefully it will be seen that one side of the V-shaped lacing pattern is worked over 2 canes and the other over 3 canes. When the mat is reversed the opposite is the case. The change from one to the other takes place at the base of the V.

FIG. 173

For instructions for lapping see Fig. 96 and text (DROP HANDLES) page 61.

To complete the circle undo the start and lap in both ends together.

Measurements:

Diameter of inner figure: 5 ins.
Diameter of finished mat: 5½ ins.

XX.   LIGHT FRAME SHOPPING BASKET   Figure 168
(Cane)

Materials:

2 lengths of Kubu (shiny handle cane) 8 mm. thick, 40 ins. and 39 ins. long.
No. 16 centre cane for 4 pairs of stakes.
¼ lb. shiny lapping cane.

A cross frame, 11 ins. × 11 ins., is needed. If this is not lap-jointed but made of one piece of wood nailed on another, the lower piece (going from side to side, that is: handle to handle) must be rather over ¼ in. longer either side, because it will be fastened there to the handle ring, which is outside the horizontal one, and not to the horizontal ring at all four points. A lap-jointed frame is preferable.

Make 2 circles, one 11 ins. in diameter and the other 11½ ins. diameter and follow Figs. 128-131 and explanatory notes on pages 72, 75 and 76.

RECIPES

XXI. OVAL FRAME-TYPE DISH — Figure 168

An introduction to frame-making and the construction of this type of basket.

Materials:

    1 piece of Kubu or 8-mm. handle cane about 30 ins. long for the frame.
    No. 12 cane for sticks.
    1 oz. flat lapping cane for weaving.
    (The whole could be made in willow with skeins for weaving.)

Construction:

    Make a slightly squared oval frame $9\frac{3}{4}$ ins. × $5\frac{1}{2}$ ins. with an overlapping join about 4 ins. at one side. It is not necessary to use a shaping board, but the frame can be kept in shape during weaving with a temporary twist across the centre.

Nail a centre stake of No. 12 on the under side from end to end, allowing for the curve. Bind it in, working from the centres first at one end and then at the other. After about 6 turns set another stake on either side of the centre one and weave that in. Finally add two more stakes. Continue to weave from each end alternately, taking a round turn over the frame after each crossing. It may be necessary to pack once or twice (see Fig. 48). Join the flat cane by laying the new end over the old one.

For a larger dish more stakes are needed.

For the *method of weaving* see Fig. 59. In this illustration the stakes are scallomed and not nailed or laid in.

5. NOTES ON THE PHOTOGRAPHS
(Figures 1–13, 112–116, 124–127, 132–139 and 141–146)

FIG. 1. The Silchester basket. *By permission of the Duke of Wellington and the Reading Museum and Art Gallery.*
Fragment of a willow basket (diameter $3\frac{3}{4}$ ins) found in a well in the Roman city of Silchester, near Reading.

FIG. 2. The pannier used by Airborne Forces. *By permission of the Imperial War Museum.* (See page 14.)

FIG. 3. A professional basketmaker working a border on a heavy white willow basket. *By permission of the Rural Industries Bureau.*

FISHING BASKETS

FIG. 4. Quarter-cran herring basket. *By permission of the Rural Industries Bureau.*
Made by Mr. Stanley Bird of Great Yarmouth. The most familiar and widely used of English fish baskets, it is a government measure and each one bears the official stamp. It will give some idea of the accuracy with which a professional basketmaker works if we indicate where the quarter-cran must be measured to conform to exact specification.

> Across top.
> Across bottom.
> Diagonal from top to bottom inside.
> Height.
> Height of bottom dome.
> Number of woods and stakes, lines of wale, etc.
> Weight finished.
> Distance between stakes must be less than the width of a thumb.

Made of white willow, wood and Kubu cane. Four of these hold a cran, approximately $3\frac{1}{2}$ cwt. Mr. Bird also makes miniatures about 6 ins. high.

FIG. 5. Arbroath traditional fish creel and baskets. *By permission of the Council of Industrial Design Scottish Committee.* From the collection of Dr. Baxter of Upper Largo.

NOTES ON THE PHOTOGRAPHS

These three specimens of the basketmaker's art were shown at the "Living Traditions" Exhibition in Edinburgh in 1951. They are frame-type baskets made of wood and fine Kubu or Palembang Cane.

FIG. 6. Scottish sculls. Behind: from Fife. In front: from the Moray Firth. *By permission of Dr. Baxter of Upper Largo.*

These baskets were once familiar all round the East Coast of Scotland, but now they are hard to find. They were used to carry coiled and baited lines for line fishing. A frame-type basket of wood and willow. Handles at the sides.

FIG. 7. Coarse fishing basket. *By permission of the Rural Industries Bureau.*
Made by Miss F. N. Hyde of Worcester. Buff willows.

FIG. 8. Fish caizie (back creel) from Orkney. *By permission of Dr. Baxter of Upper Largo.*

A true primitive woven of heather stalks and roots on the island of Orkney. It proves that a basket may be made of any growing material that is available. In Miss Baxter's collection of Scottish baskets is another back creel made of docken stalks woven with bents, from Shetland.

FIG. 9. Fly-fishing creel. *By permission of the Rural Industries Bureau.*
Made by Mr. A. Hembrow of Glastonbury. The shape of this traditional basket is familiar but beautifully functional. The back curves in to fit the body when it is carried.

FIG. 10. The Yarmouth herring swill.
Made by Mr. Stanley Bird of Great Yarmouth. This magnificent primitive has three handles and is made of brown willow and hazel. It is peculiar to Great Yarmouth and three will carry a cran of herring, each a two-man load. The system of using swills is complicated. They are always stacked on the quay in threes, in a pyramid. Four quarter-crans (Fig. 4) fill three swills: one fills the top swill and the other three the bottom swills. This makes the top swill easier to lift. Empty swills are carried by the central handle.

FIGS. 11 and 12. Eel traps. *By permission of the Rural Industries Bureau.*
Fig. 11 is made by Mr. Alfred James of Welney, Norfolk, of hazel.
Fig. 12 is made by Mr. Stanley Bird of Great Yarmouth, of willow rods.
These curious marvels might be totems and certainly the design must belong to the earliest marsh-dwelling people.

AGRICULTURAL BASKETS

FIG. 13. Potato basket. Monmouth. *By permission of the Rural Industries Bureau.*
Perfect craftsmanship has made a utilitarian object both graceful and

NOTES ON THE PHOTOGRAPHS

strong. This type of basket is found all over Europe. White willow and hazel.

FIG. 112. Welsh garden basket. *By permission of the Rural Industries Bureau.*

Pretty enough for that embroiderer's myth, the Crinoline Lady? There is nothing feminine about its construction, and it will act as a scoop for vegetables or fruit. White willow and hazel, the edge bound with wire.

FIG. 113. Malt skip. *By permission of the Rural Industries Bureau.*

Made by Mr. W. Shelley of Salisbury, in white willow. It is used for shovelling barley.

FIG. 114. Huck-muck or barrel strainer. *By permission of the Rural Industries Bureau.*

Made by Mr. W. Shelley of Salisbury, in white willow. Used in the days when the small man could brew his own beer. It fitted over the tap inside the barrel and when the tap was turned the beer strained through the huck-muck. About 9 ins. high.

FIG. 115. Deep fruit picker. *By permission of the Rural Industries Bureau.*

Made by Mr. Harrison of St. Ives, Hunts, of white and brown willow. Baskets of this type are familiar to all who live in a fruit-growing area.

TRADE AND DOMESTIC

FIG. 116. Oval shopper. *By permission of the Rural Industries Bureau.*

Made by Mr. Finch of Gloucester, in brown and white willow, with a scalloped base.

FIG. 124. Egg basket. *By permission of the Rural Industries Bureau.*

Made by Mr. W. Shelley of Salisbury, in buff willow. The entire side of this basket is made with the stakes. Many baskets of this type are made in Italy and Madeira and, indeed, it is a universal method but not suitable where great strength is needed.

FIG. 125. Cat basket. *By permission of the Rural Industries Bureau.*

Made by Mr. A. Hembrow of Glastonbury, of buff willow. Height 12 ins.

A basketmaker will always make a basket to fit an individual dog or cat. Dachshunds, for instance, dislike draughts and appreciate a complete hood over them.

FIG. 126. Bottle basket. *By permission of the Rural Industries Bureau.*

Made by Mr. Blackall of Chasney Bassett, Wantage, in buff and white willow. Baskets of this type vary in shape and size to suit the different trades which use them. The partitions are made after the basket is completed and then tied in.

NOTES ON THE PHOTOGRAPHS

FIG. 127. Log basket. *By permission of the Rural Industries Bureau.*

Made by Mr. A. Hembrow of Glastonbury, in white and brown willow. The lovely curve of this basket is typical of Mr. Hembrow's work, but there is strength as well as grace.

FIG. 132. The Skye hen or ose basket. *By permission of* The Farmer's Weekly.

White willow skein. The fashion basket of the year not only in the British Isles but also in Europe. The origin of this basket is uncertain. Some say it originated in Scandinavia—but in Sweden they call it the Scottish basket—others say in Hungary, though the ones coming from there and Yugoslavia are more elongated and always made in buff willow. There is another rumour that a similar basket has been used in Sicily for years for fish.

Whatever its origin it was the basketmakers of Kilmuir in Skye who developed it here. It has been used in the Isles and the Western Highlands for some years but caught the public eye when it was shown at the "Living Traditions" Exhibition in Edinburgh in 1951. Now a few English basketmakers make it too.

Its old use in Scotland was for carrying a broody hen from one croft to another, when before the days of incubators it was the custom to borrow a broody hen from a neighbour. "Ose" comes from osier, or willow. It is a difficult basket, even for a skilled man until he knows it, and emphatically should not be copied by amateurs in centre cane.

FIG. 133. Work basket. *By permission of the Rural Industries Bureau.*

Made by Miss F. N. Hyde of Worcester. A beautiful example of fine buff willow work made by a professional woman basketmaker who comes from an old basketmaking family.

FIG. 134. Shoe basket. Hebrides. *By permission of Primavera, London.*

White willow skein. The name of this basket would appear to refer to its shape rather than its use, which is for holding eggs.

FIG. 135. Tray. *By permission of Primavera, London.*

Buff willow. Made by Mr. W. Shelley of Salisbury.

FIG. 136. Tea basket. *By permission of the Rural Industries Bureau.*

Made by Mr. W. H. Sandling of Stroud, in buff willow. It measures 7 ins. × 20 ins. × 14 ins. and is a typical rectangular willow basket. More elaborate picnic baskets have trunk covers, and fastenings vary according to type and price.

FIG. 137. Creelagh. *By permission of Dr. Baxter of Upper Largo.*

This curious object from the Highlands and Islands of Scotland was used for holding carded wool when spinning. It is about 15 ins. long and stoutly made of hazel and brown willow.

Fig. 138. Birdcage. *By permission of the Rural Industries Bureau.*

Made by Mr. Leslie Maltby of Kensington in white willow. Country people used to keep blackbirds and starlings in such cages and would put their food on the little square platform at the side. Nowadays they can hold a light in the porch or hang full of herbs in a kitchen window.

Fig. 139. Cradle. *Crown copyright reserved, reproduced by permission of the Controller, H.M. Stationery Office.*

This buff willow cradle is a Government basket, made to specification for the use of the children of service personnel. It is a fine example of fitching. It measures 33 ins. × 18 ins. at the top; $26\frac{1}{2}$ ins. × 14 ins. at the bottom; $14\frac{1}{2}$ ins. height of head; 12 ins. height of foot.

TOYS

Fig. 141. Willow rattle. *By permission of Primavera, London.*

Made from six 3-ft., thin, white willow rods with the kindest nature and as near as possible the same thickness for the greater part of their length. The principle of construction is the same as a corn dolly and the rattle is not difficult to make. The perfect willow rods are the problem.

About $4\frac{1}{2}$ ins. long, with a bell or two pieces of tin inside.

Fig. 142. Doll's chairs and sofa. *By permission of Primavera, London.*

Made of buff willow.

Fig. 143. Doll's cradle. *By permission of Primavera, London.*

Made in buff willow.

EXAMPLES OF DOUBTFUL DESIGN

Fig. 144. Plant pot holders.

Four specimens of a multitude of "contemporary" designs. Those at the sides are neo-Victoria, while the centre ones are not baskets at all. Perhaps this should be called the "gimmick" school of basketry.

Fig. 145. The Gainsborough.

High fashion in 1900, but it looks very odd with present-day furniture.

At its best the design is not bad; at its worst, spray-painted in colour and gold, with the lip over-enlarged and pulled out of shape, it is very ugly. But every horticultural show and many flower shops use it to display everything from chrysanthemums to cauliflowers.

Fig. 146. Cane frame shopper.

Baskets like this one are made in thousands, yet they are never cheap, and always more expensive than willow ones. Usually both coloured plastic

NOTES ON THE PHOTOGRAPHS

and dyed cane are used and seldom match. Sometimes there is raffia embroidery, sometimes not, but it never bears any relation to the design.

The basket is bulky but does not hold a lot. This one cost 22s. 6d. at a south-west London store which prides itself on serving persons of taste.

It should be said that many of these baskets are partially made by the blind and disabled, but this is no excuse. They have been designed by professional sighted basketmakers and would appear to have been inspired by a German pattern book 25 years old.

This one weighs 1 lb. 6 ozs. and measures 13 ins. × 7½ ins. × 6 ins. Compare it with the one in Fig. 158 which weighs 13½ ozs. and is larger.

6. BASKETMAKER'S VOCABULARY

Back: the convex side of a willow rod.
Belly: the whole basket after the border is worked. Also the concave side of a willow rod.
Border: the finishing edge of the sides, lid or foot of a basket, made by bringing the stakes down and weaving them into a set pattern.
Bow or Bow-rod: the bent willow or cane forming the centre of a handle.
Bow-mark: a short rod the thickness of a handle put where the handle will be and worked over during the making of a basket. Withdrawn when the handle is put in.
Butt: the thick end of a willow rod.
Bye-stake: a stake not inserted into the base. (Is sometimes used instead of the term "liner".)
Cram: a sharpened stake turned down at right angles, sometimes used in finishing a willow border.
Fitching: open-work in cane or willow basketry, formed with the stakes in the fabric of the basket, not in bordering.
Fitch-pairing: the reverse twist of pairing, used when fitching.
Foot: a border worked on the bottom of a basket or the method of joining stakes to a wooden base with holes.
Hoop: a ring formed by coiling a rod upon itself and used to hold the stakes upright while the upsett, and in some cases the belly, is being worked. Also used of the ring frame used in scallomed work.
Lapping: binding with skein willow or flat cane.
League: bottom stick and stakes are in one continuous rod.
Ledge: a small shelf worked on the inside of a basket on which a lid drops in and rests.
Liner: a rod inserted by the side of a stake for strength or decorative effect. (Sometimes called a "bye-stake".)
Listing: a decorative pattern worked with additional skeins or flat cane when lapping a handle.
Osier: another name for willow.
Pairing: two canes worked alternately over and under each other, forming a twist.
Picking: cutting off the projecting ends of rods when a basket is completed. (A base may be picked after completion before the belly is worked.)

BASKETMAKER'S VOCABULARY

Pricking-up: turning up of willow stakes over the point of the knife after they have been inserted into the base. In a cane basket the stakes are squeezed with round-nosed pliers.

Rand: a single rod worked in front of one stake and behind the next.

Rib-rand: one rod worked in front of two stakes and behind one. The total of stakes should *not* divide by three.

Rods: Willows used in the craft of basketmaking or single lengths of cane.

Round: one complete circular movement made round a basket, lid or base.

Scallom: method of fixing stakes to a ring of willow or cane.

Skein: a strip of the outer part of a willow rod.

Slath: the structure made by the bottom sticks of a base.

Slew: two or more rods worked together in front of one stake and behind the next.

Slype: a slanting or flat cut.

Spale: thin strips of wood such as oak or chestnut woven into a basket; sometimes used as stakes or sticks with other materials as weaving.

Stakes: rods driven in with the bottom sticks to form the foundation of the sides of a basket.

Sticks: short lengths of willow or cane forming the foundation of a base or lid.

Stroke: a movement in basketmaking like a stitch in sewing or knitting.

Top or *tip:* the thin end of a willow rod.

Trac: a simple border worked with one stake, or a stake and its liner, at a time.

Trunk Cover: a lid that fits over a basket.

Upsett: the setting-up of the sides of a basket, usually employing a round of 4- or 5-rod waling and several rows of 3-rod. The most important part of any basket since the shape springs from it.

Wale: three or more rods worked in sequence in front of two, three or more stakes and behind one. Or in front of two or three and behind two, using four or five rods.

Weaver: the length of willow or cane used in the weaving of a basket as opposed to a stake round which it is woven.

Withe: another name for willow.

7. BOOKS

FOR THE WORKER:
Canework, Charles Crampton. 10/6d. Dryad Press.
Willow Basketry, A J. Knock. 3s. Dryad Press.
Simple Basketry, Mabel Roffey. 7/6d. Pitman.
Basketry the Easy Way, O. R. Scott. 7/6d. Central Press Pty. Ltd., Sydney. (Cane only.)
* *La Vannerie* (Basketmaking), R. Duchesne, H. Ferrand and J. Thomas. 1953. Approx. 25s. J-B. Balliére et Fils, Paris. (In French, but the illustrations are easy to follow. A complete encyclopaedia including regional baskets and furniture.)
* *Handbok i Korgflätnung* (Handbook of Basketmaking), Erland Borgland and Thure Hyllén. 17/6d. LTs Förlag. Stockholm. (In Swedish but with beautiful clear drawings and photographs, mostly of willow baskets.)
† *The Art of Basketmaking*, Thomas Okey. Pitman.
† *Lehrbuch für Korbflechter* (Manual of Basketmaking), Gustav Funke. 1903. Denticke, Vienna.
† *The Basketmaker*, Luther Weston Turner. New York. 1909.
Basic Basketry, Leonard G. Allbon. 21/–. Max Parrish.

HISTORICAL AND HORTICULTURAL:
Basketry Through the Ages, H. H. Bobart. Oxford 1936. 10/6d, from Heffer, Cambridge
† *Records of the Basketmakers' Company*, H. H. Bobart. Dunn Collin & Co.
Cultivation and Uses of Basket Willows, K. G. Stott, B.Sc., Willow Officer, University of Bristol Research Station, Long Ashton. Reprinted from the *Quarterly Journal of Forestry*, April, 1956. (Obtainable from Long Ashton.)
† *Rural Industries of England and Wales*, Vols. II and IV, H. H. Peach. Oxford.
– *Household Country Crafts*, Alan Jobson. (Elek) 1953.
Living Crafts, G. Bernard Hughes. 15s. Lutterworth. 1953.
Made in England, Dorothy Hartley. 16s. Methuen. 1940.

BOOKS

† *Woodland Crafts in Britain*, H. L. Edlin. 1949. Batsford.
† *Indian Basketry*, Geo. Wharton James. 1903. New York.
† *Poetry and Symbolism of Indian Basketry*, Geo. Wharton James. Pasadena.
† *Indian Basketry*, Otis Tufton Mason. 2 vols. Heinemann.

* Obtainable through London booksellers specialising in Continental books.
† Out of print. Available in some libraries.

APPENDIX A

Dyeing for Basket Makers

THE following dyes which are recommended by the I.C.I. for dyeing cane, willow, seagrass and raffia are extremely fast when used either separately or in mixtures. They are obtainable by post from Messrs. Skilbeck Bros. Ltd., 55, Glengall Road, London, S.E.15, but care must be taken when ordering to quote the number given after the dye.

Dye	Cost per lb. excluding postage, January, 1963		
	£	s.	d.
Methylene Blue 2B150		16	9
Auramine ON.150 (yellow)		13	9
Chrysoidine T.160 (orange)		13	9
Methyl Violet 2B200		14	6
Rhodamine B.500 (crimson)	1	12	6
Malachite Green Crystals		14	–

Available in 1-lb. amounts.

DIRECTIONS FOR DYEING CANE, WILLOW, SEAGRASS, RAFFIA:

The following table gives the amount of dye and water, also the time of immersion.

APPENDIX A

No.	Dyes used	Quantity (level measures)	Gallons of water	Time of boiling (minutes)
1.	Methyl violet 2B200. Violet	1	2	5
2.	Rhodamine B500 } Purple Methylene blue 2B150	{ 3 { 1	4	5
3.	Methylene blue 2B150. Blue	1	2	5
4.	Methylene blue 2B150 } Turquoise Malachite green YS crystals	{ 1 { 1	4	5
5.	Malachite green YS crystals. Blue-green	1	2	5
6.	Auramine ON.150 } Emerald green Malachite green YS crystals	{ 1 { 1	4	10
7.	Auramine ON.150 } Yellow-green Malachite green YS crystals	{ 3 { 1	4	5
8.	Auramine ON.150. Yellow	2	1	5
9.	Chrysoidine Y160. Orange	1	2	5
10.	Rhodamine B500 } A clear scarlet Auramine ON.150	{ 1 { 3	2	5
11.	Rhodamine B500 } A dark claret Chrysoidine Y160	{ 1 { 1	2	10
12.	Rhodamine B500. Crimson	1	1	5

APPENDIX A

1. The required amount of dye powder should be carefully measured and dissolved in a little boiling water. Use a clean measure and dye bath.
2. The rest of the water should be added and raised to boiling point.
3. Completely immerse the material to be dyed for the time stated.
4. Move the material about gently whilst it is in the dye bath.
5. Wash the material well in cold water immediately after dyeing.
6. Hang out to dry.

The standard measure is approximately 9 grains of dye powder, that is as much as will lie, lightly heaped, on a sixpence.

NOTES:
(i) Paler colours may be obtained by adding more water.
(ii) The amount of dye soluble in 1 gallon of water is enough to dye approximately 1 lb. of material.
(iii) Care should be taken when using these dyes. They are much stronger than household dyes, and even a pinch in 1 pint of water is enough to dye 2 ozs. of material.
(iv) On the other hand they do not stain an enamel bowl, and dye can easily be removed from it with scouring powder.
(v) Experiments in colour mixing can be made in a cup, trying out tiny quantities of the powders and noting results on sticks of cane or willow.
(vi) Bleached cane, besides giving a clearer colour, takes the dye more evenly than natural cane. Do not try to dye buff willow.
(vii) Never add salt.

INDEX

The numerals in **heavy type** refer to the *figure numbers* of the illustrations

Agricultural baskets, 130; **13, 112-15**
Airborne panniers, 17, 129; **2**
All-purpose plate, 113; **159**
Amateurs, 18, 80, 89
Arbroath creels, 129; **5**

Ball, cane, 125; **167**
Barrel-strainer or huck-muck, 131; **114**
Bases, 42 *et seq.*
   design of a round, 91
   design of an oval, 92; **148-150**
   frame, 45; **59**
   oval, 43, 45; **56, 57**
   randed, 42, 43; **54, 55**
   rectangular, 35, 45; **58**
   round, 41-43; **49-55**
   wooden, 46, 50, 57, 93; **92**
Basket, design of an actual, 90 *et seq.*; **147-151**
Basketmakers' Company, 17
Basketmaking Industry, 13-14, 17-18, 21
   blind and disabled workers, 17
   difficulties, 14, 21
   early records, 17
   future, 18-21, 79
   history of, 13-14, 17
   organisations connected with, 18
   rates for work, 14
   training, 14
   war record, 17
Baxter, Miss E. M., 129, 130, 132
Bird, Mr. Stanley, 129, 130
Birdcage, 133; **138**
Blackall, Mr., 131
Blind workers, **17**, 134
Boat-shaped oval basket, 93
Bobart, *Basketry through the Ages*, 137
Bodkins, 30; **15 16, 17**
Books on Basketry, List of, 137
Borders, 47 *et seq.*
   five-pair plait, 56; **84-89**
   foot border, 57; **92**

four-pair plait, 56
four-rod plain, 54; **77**
madeira-type, 56; **90, 91**
on lids, 65
plait on side, 56
roll, 50
scallop, 47; **65-67**
trac, 47-50, 66; **68-70**
three-pair plait, 54; **78-83**
three-rod plain, 50; **71-74**
with back-trac, 52; **76**
with follow-on trac, 52; **75**
working a, 129; **3**
Bottle basket, 131; **126**
Bow, 135
   marks, 64, 135
Bowl, bread or fruit, 124; **166**
Bradawl, 30; **28**
Butt, 135; **14**
Bye-stakes, 65, 135; **109**

Caizie, Fish, 130; **8**
Cane, 27, 80, 86, 89
   bleaching, 29, 141
   dyeing, 86, 139 *et seq.*
   grading and quality, 29
   handles, 49 *et seq.*; **93-107**
   marketing, 28
   preparation of, 29
   processing, 28
   recipes for making baskets, etc., 99-128; **152-168**
   spirit lamp, 30; **25**
   tools, 30; **15-28**
   varnishing, 86
Carpet beater, 123; **165**
Cat basket, 131; **125**
Chair cane, 28, 29, 60, 70
Changing-the-stroke, 37, 38-40; **40-42**
"Chasing", 35; **34**
Cleave, 33; **29**
Closed notch, 71; **120**
Clothes pegs, 33
Colour, 38, 40, 57, 86, 89, 93, 139 *et seq.*
   recipes using, 99, 101, 102, 113, 120, 125, 126; **153, 154, 155, 160, 164, 167**
Council of Industrial Design, 129

Cradle, 93, 133; **139**
   miniature, 122; **165**
Cram, 50, 135
Creels, 17, 129, 130; **5, 8, 9**
Creelagh, 132; **137**

Decorative weaves, 40, 59
Denmark, 79
Design,
   bad, 79, 89, 133, 134; **144, 145, 146**
   colour in, 86, 88, 93, 139 *et seq.*
   craftsmanship, 89
   "Contemporary", 79; **144**
   "Do-it-yourself", 80
   finish, 89, 90
   from pottery, 85
   material, right use of, 89
   need for more up-to-date, 79
   of actual baskets, 90 *et seq.*; **147-151**
   proportion in, 94
   shape, 85
   strength, 80
   taste, 85
   texture, 86
Disabled workers, 17, 134
Dish, interlaced, 126; **167**
   oval frame-type, 128; **168**
Dog baskets, 66, 131
Doll's chair and sofa, 133; **142**
   cradle, 133; **143**
Dyeing, 86, 130 *et seq.*

East Anglia, 22, 26
Eel traps, 89, 130; **11, 12**
Egg basket, 131; **124**
Enamelled cane, 86

Far Eastern basketry, 85
Finch, Mr., 131
Fish baskets and measures, 17, 129; **4**
Fishing baskets, 129; **4-12**
Fitch or reverse pairing, 39, 135; **47**
Fitching, 135

142

INDEX

Florist's basket, 79, 133; **145**
Fly-fishing creel, 130; **9**
Fruit bowl, 124; **166**
  picker, 131; **115**

Gainsborough, The, 79, 133, **145**
Germany, 26, 28, 29, 131

Hammer, 30; **24**
Handles, 58 et seq., 76, 80, 93; 93-107
  dropped, 61; **100, 101**
  dropped ring, 61; **102**
  lapped, 59, 80; **95**
  leather, 116, 120; **154, 161, 164**
  listed, crossed, 60; **99**
  listed, herringbone, 59; **97, 98**
  pegging of, 59, 95
  roped, 58; **93, 94**
  Turk's Head 12, 61; **103-107**
Hembrow, Mr., 130, 131, 132
Herring cran, 129; **4**
Herring swill, Yarmouth, 130; **10**
Hoop, 46, 135; **61**
Huck-muck or barrel strainer, 131; **114**
Hungary, 26, 132
Hyde, Miss F. N., 130, 132

Imported baskets, 17, 80
Interlaced dish, 126; **167**
  mat, 126; **167**
Italian basketware, 79, 85, 86

James, Mr. Alfred, 130
Jam-jar, 33

Knife, 30; **20**
Kubu cane, 27, 72, 127, 129, 130

Lapping, 59, 61, 135; **95, 96**
Leach, Bernard, 89
League, 44, 135; **56**
Leather handles, 101, 120; **154, 164**
  harness, 116, **161**
Ledges, 64; **109, 110**
Lidded picnic basket, 114, **161**
Lids, 36, 64-66; **108**

Light frame shopping basket, 127; **168**
Linen baskets, 86, 94, 118; **163**
Liners, 65, 92, 135
Listing, 59-61, 135; **97-99**
"Living Traditions" Exhibition, Edinburgh, 130, 132
Log basket, 132; **127**

Malacca cane, 27
Malt skip, 131; **113**
Maltby, Mr. Leslie, 133
Mat, interlaced, 126; **167, 173**
Military use, baskets for, 17, 129
Miniature carpet beater, 124; **165**
  cradle, 122; **165**
  round shopping basket, 123; **165**
Moulds, canework over wooden, 85

Nails, 30
Napkin ring, 64
Notches, 66, 69-71; **117-120, 162**

Okey, Thomas (qu.), The Art of Basketmaking, 27, 137
Opening-out, 42; **52, 54, 55, 56**
Osier, 22, 135

Packing, 40; **48**
Pairing, 39, 40, 42, 135; **46, 47, 51, 52**
  chain, 39; **47**
  fitch-or reverse, 39; **47**
Palembang cane, 27, 29, 75, 86, 130
Pannier rustique, 72
Pegging, 59, 80; **95**
Picking, 135
  knife, 34; **32**
Picnic baskets, 80, 114; **161**
Plaiting five rods, 71; **123**
Plant-pot holders, 133; **144**
Plastic cane, 86, 133
Plate, all-purpose, 113; **159**
  Swedish, 113; **160**
Pliers, round-nosed, 30; **18**
  long-nosed, 30
Potato basket, Monmouth, 130; **13**
Pricking-up, 46, 136; **61**

Primavera, 132, 133
Quarter-cran herring basket, 129; **4**

Raffia, dyeing of, 139 et seq.
Randing, 34-36; **33, 34, 54-56**
  french, 36; **36**
  rib, 36, 66, 135; **37**
Rapping iron, 30; **22**
Rattan cane, 28
Rattle, cane, 125; **166**
  willow, 133; **141**
Recipes, 99 et seq.; **152-168**
Reed (American), 28
Round basket, Design of, 90, 91; **147**
  frame basket, Construction of, 72-76, 127; **128-131, 168**
Ruler, 30, 89; **23**
Rural Industries Bureau, 129, 131, 133
Rush baskets, 86

Sandling, Mr. W. H., 132
Sarawak cane, 27
Scallom, 45, 136; **59**
Scallop, 47, 94; **65-67**
Scandinavia, 79
Scotland, basketry in, 17, 129, 130
Screw block, 30, 45; **26, 58**
Scull, Scottish, 130; **6**
Seagrass, dyeing of, 139 et seq.
"Sea mat", 126; **172**
Secateurs, 30; **19**
Selotape, 33
Shaping board, 45; **60**
Sharpening stone, 33

Shave, 33; **30**
Shelley, Mr. W., 131, 132
Shetland, 130
Shoe basket, 132; **134**
Shopping baskets, 56, 58, 102, 103, 120, 123, 127, 131, 133; **116, 146, 155, 158, 164, 168**
Side cutters, 30; **21**
Silchester basket, 129; **1**
Skein, 33, 86, 136; **29**
Skeining, 25, 27
Skye hen or ose basket, 132; **132**
Slath, 42, 135; **49-57**
  design of, 91; **148-151**
Slewing, 35, 90, 135; **35**

143

INDEX

Slype, 136
Slyped overlap, 46; **59, 62**
Soap, 33
Somerset, 22
Spale, 79, 136
Stakes, 46, 90, 136; **61-64**
   into a rectangular woven base, 47; **63, 64**
Staking-up, 46, 92; **61-64, 151**
Sticks, 42, 136; **49-57**
Straw plait, 86
String, 33
Strokes, *see* Weaves
Sweden, 79, 132
Swedish plate, 113; **160**

Tallow, **33**
Tea basket, 132; **136**
Ties and Trimmings, 71 *et seq.* 75, 93; **121-123, 130, 131**
Tohiti cane, 27
Tools, cane, 30, 33; **15-28** willow, 33; **29-32**
Toys, willow, 133; **141-143** cane, 122, 123, 125; **165-167**
Trac borders, 47-52, 57, 94; **68-70, 75, 76, 92**
Trade and Domestic Baskets, 131 *et seq.*; **116, 124-127, 132-139**

Trays, 50, 132; **135**
Trunk covers, 65, 101, 114, 136; **154, 161**
Turk's Head, 61; **103-107**
Upright, 33; **31**
Upsetting, 46, 47, 85, 136; **62, 140**
Ur, Mesopotamia, 12

Vocabulary, Basketmaker's, 135

Waling, 36-38, 40, 46, 90, 136; **37-45, 62**
   chain, 38; **44**
   changing-the-stroke in, 37, 39, 40; **40-42**
   double-chain, 38
   five-rod, 38, 46, 65; **62**
   four-rod, 38, 57; **43**
   over a core, 47; **62**
   three-rod, 36, 40, 66; **37**

Waste-paper basket, 99; **152**
Weavers, 90, 136
Weaves, 34-40, 93; **33-48**, *see* Randing, Waling, etc.
   Decorative, 40
Weights, 30

Welsh garden basket, 131; **112**
Whangee cane, 27
Willow, 10, 13, 14, 17, 21, 22, 80, 86; **14**
   commercial baskets, 129-133; **3, 4, 6, 7, 9-13, 112-116, 124-127, 132-139**
   cultivation, 25
   handles, 58
   important, 26
   preparation for working, 26
   processing and marketing, 25
   rattle, 133; **141**
   recipes using some, 101-103, 113; **154, 155, 158, 160**
   tools, 33; **29-32**
Wine cradle, 66, 116; **59, 162**
Women's and Evening Institutes, 18, 80
Wooden bases, *see* Bases
   recipes for baskets on, 99, 116, 118; **152, 162, 163**
Workbaskets, 100, 101, 132; **133, 153, 154**
Workboard, 30; **27**

Yarmouth herring swill, 130; **10**
Yugo-Slavia, 132